BACKYARD MEAT RABBITS FOR BEGINNERS

YOUR QUICK AND CONCISE GUIDE TO EFFORTLESSLY
RAISE RABBITS

MEAT ON YOUR TABLE IN AS LITTLE AS 90 DAYS!

ANNE MCKENZIE

CONTENTS

INTRODUCTION

WHY RAISE RABBITS?

For years my husband and I have said that rabbits are an untapped resource. Many people simply don't realize their potential impact and value.

Rabbits can be an economical source of meat. These docile, sensitive animals are perfectly suited to small-scale and urban farming and have provided many households with sustainable and hormone-free, meat. Rabbit meat is a natural choice. It's low in cholesterol and calories, rich in clean protein, and promotes heart health. As a bonus, rabbit meat production is friendlier to the environment when compared to other meat products.

As a country girl, small-scale farmer, wife, and mother of six, I want to provide my family with the best nourishment possible. With one buck and two does, a breeder can easily produce 192 lbs of processed rabbit meat, or 300 lbs of live-weight meat if bred vigorously. Rabbits are known to be vigorous breeders, so this is an easy feat for them!

I have a long history with rabbits. My family had rabbits when I was a child. Little did I know that halfway around the world my future husband (at seven years old) was also raising meat rabbits and assisting in the butchering process. Many years later, while living in Uganda, my husband and I raised meat rabbits again.

There are many reasons rabbits are a great choice for your family.

Rabbit manure makes an excellent fertilizer. It can be used directly on gardens, without letting it sit and decompose, as you would have to do with other animal manures.

Rabbits require very little infrastructure and can be raised in old chicken coops or garden sheds and cages and hutches can often be obtained second-hand or built on your own. Breeders can earn extra income by raising meat rabbits as they require comparatively less money, space, labor and time to get started.

Their small size makes them easy to handle—even the Flemish Giant maxes out at 22 lbs. Unlike larger livestock that requires permanent infrastructure, everything aspiring rabbit handlers need to raise a herd can fit into a U-Haul. Their low barrier to entry makes raising rabbits a solid starter enterprise and a well-managed rabbitry can save homesteaders money in a matter of weeks.

In this book, you will find the answers to many of your questions relating to raising, housing, breeding, butchering, and feeding rabbits in these chapters. For the beginner, you will be well prepared for all that you may encounter in your rabbit raising.

Journey with me, as we take the first steps towards getting a successful rabbitry started.

CHOOSING A HOME FOR YOUR RABBITS

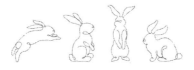

There's nothing quite as satisfying as growing your own organic vegetables and raising chemical-free meats. The secret to raising healthy rabbits is a clean-living environment. Before you can bring rabbits home, you need to have a suitable area to house them. As with all things in life, the pros and cons depends on the methods you decide to use. Your biggest initial expectation will be the housing units or cages for your rabbits, but if you take care to plan it properly, you will find that a well-made unit should last for several years.

In this chapter, I won't give plans on building your own hutch, cage, run, or enclosure. I focus primarily on the various methods and how you can make the right choice for you. Every breeder's situation, skill set, budget, and desires are individual to themselves. Should you choose to build your own rabbitry blueprints and plans are widely available on the internet. I trust that you will be able to find the design best suited to your needs. If you are on a tight budget often rabbit hutches and cages can be purchased second-hand locally.

CONSIDERATIONS BEFORE BUYING YOUR FIRST CAGE

Before you buy a cage, it is important to decide on a location first. Select a spot that offers protection from the elements. Rabbits easily overheat so a breeder's first line of defense against the heat is a simple one: keep the rabbitry in a shady, well-ventilated area. Sometimes hutches are added as an addition to the side of a barn, workshop, or shed to give the rabbits adequate protection. Keeping a rabbitry near the home may also protect rabbits from predators.

When laying plans for the rabbitry, make sure that you provide them with enough space. A cage measuring 2–3ft. on the inside is suitable for smaller breeds and 5ft. for medium-sized breeds. Giant breeds will require a space of 6–8ft. inside their cages. Use these measurements as guidelines to help you select or build big enough housing.

Beginners, especially if you have limited space, are advised to start with smaller to medium-sized breeds. Giant rabbit breeds tend to be pricey, but if they suit your plans, budget, and space available, go for it. The depth of a smaller cage should be no more than 3ft. to allow easy access to the rabbits. Larger cages can be deeper as needed. If you opt for a storied solution to house rabbits, keep in mind that there should be a tray to catch droppings beneath the second floor. Keep in mind that the more levels the rabbit housing complex have, the harder it becomes to keep it clean and adequately ventilated.

Rabbits, just like people, need a daily dose of sunshine for vitamin D. If your rabbits are housed indoors, this situation can be easily remedied by adding vitamin D supplements to their feed. Additionally, you'll need to provide nest boxes for the animals. Wooden fruit boxes are commonly used as birthing beds. The bed should be lined with a clean, absorbent material like straw, sawdust, cotton hulls, or wood shavings, though never use cedar shavings, which could pose a danger to your rabbit's health.

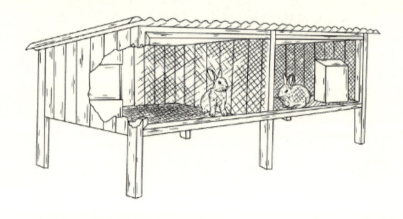

TRADITIONAL HUTCH CAGE

This is a common type of housing that provides a comfortable and easy-to-access home for rabbits. Ideally, the front of the hutch and one or two sides of the cage should be covered in heavy wire, that way the rabbits get enough ventilation and remain protected from predators. Wire-fronted doors should hang on dependable buckles or latches. The floor of the unit should also be wired to allow droppings to fall through. Avoid using chicken wire as flooring as it is too fine and can be hard on the rabbit's feet, especially in breeds that don't have a lot of padding. Hutches should be free from sharp edges and jagged pieces of wire that may cause injury to the animals.

The remaining solid walls can be made from wood, but keep in mind that rabbits love to gnaw. Use heavy, untreated wood in any areas the animals will have access to. You can discourage gnawing by providing your rabbits with a freshly cut branch of edible wood such as a fruit branch. Change it as often as needed to keep their interest and extend the lifespan of the hutch. If gnawing remains a problem, it is best to cover vulnerable spots with a cheap and pliable metal like tin sheeting. The hutch should be built on legs to protect the rabbits from dampness and droppings that gather on the soil below. Every good hutch needs a solid roof. Canvas or plastic tarps are suitable for warmer climates, but if you live in a cold climate a roof made from wood will be more suitable.

Benefits of Hutches

Hutches can keep rabbits from harming each other. Even though rabbits are social animals, there are occasions when they might fight and bite each other, so hutches can help to reduce stress caused by territorial animals. Other benefits include.

- Streamlining the care process.
- Ensures no accidental breeding takes place.
- Easy to prepare for the arrival of kits.

- Dead kits and rabbits can easily be removed from hutch enclosures.
- Hutches are suitable to use in urban environments or if space is limited.
- Keeps rabbits safe from predators.
- Prevents contact with wild rabbits.
- Rabbits are unlikely to escape from a well-designed hutch.

Drawbacks of Hutch Housing

You may notice that it is harder to see your rabbits in a hutch. Rabbits are shy and may spend more time in their sleeping boxes when kept in a hutch. Other drawbacks include:

- *Dark Interiors:* While rabbits prefer mid-light conditions (dusk and dawn), some hutches can be too dark for the rabbits to be comfortable.
- *Damage:* Weather can damage an outdoor hutch pretty quickly if the materials are not of high quality, leaving your rabbits in danger of exposure and predators.
- *Tight Fit:* Hutches can be too small for the needs of some rabbit breeds. When a rabbit is kept in a hutch that is too small, health problems can arise and the animal can develop back problems and pain as a result.

- *Harder To Socialize:* Rabbits need to socialize with other rabbits, but hutches do not always provide enough space for this to happen. Rabbits can get frustrated in tight quarters, which may lead to fights and injuries in the herd.
- *Sore Hocks:* Poorly designed hutch enclosures can contribute to sore hocks, especially when not enough resting boards are made available.
- *Muscle Tone Not as Developed:* When raising rabbits in a pen, colony setting, or run, they tend to develop better muscle tone, resulting in trim and healthy rabbits. Rabbits confined to a hutch may not have enough space to adequately run and play. This sedentary lifestyle may make them more susceptible to health issues in the long term.

Which Cage Wire Should I Use to Build Rabbit Enclosures?

Galvanized wire is the best to use. Try to use 14 gauge if available. For the flooring, it is best to use half-inch by one-inch wire. The top and sides can be constructed with wire measuring one by two inches.

COLONY RAISING

When raising animals, there is a long-standing belief that it is ideal to work within the animal's natural instincts. Many rabbits are social animals, in the wild rabbits live in colonies that can number anywhere from a few individuals to a couple of dozen rabbits. In the colony, they graze, snuggle to keep warm, keep a lookout for predators, and practice social grooming. It is an attractive option for those who want to raise animals in more natural environments.

Benefits of Colony Raising

Colony raising may prove to be a good option for breeders who don't have a lot of time to spare. Other benefits of colony raising include.

- Cleanup is relatively easy.
- With the added freedom, rabbits are often happier and more relaxed.
- Rabbits can dig burrows to keep warm or cool.
- Giving the rabbits food and water is easier and faster.
- Rabbits live in a more natural environment and have improved muscle tone.
- The initial setup cost is cheaper.

- A doe can possibly be in more control of her own breeding.

Colony Raising Disadvantages

Breeders may notice that the animals become more skittish and act like wild rabbits in a colony setting. This can make catching and separating rabbits challenging. Other drawbacks include.

- The colony setting takes up more space on the breeder's property.
- Unrestrained breeding may occur if the rabbits are not separated.
- Fighting may occur.
- Rabbits may become more susceptible to diseases and illnesses can spread easier.
- Does will need adequate nesting material.

Keeping Colony Rabbits Calm

When raising rabbits in a colony, there are two things we need to look out for: fighting and unwanted breeding. We can expect a little bit of "bickering" when first introducing a new rabbit into the colony. This is natural as the rabbits need to establish where everyone fits in the pecking order. Sometimes, rabbits take to each other without any fighting at all, it really depends on the animals' temperament. Rabbits that have lived as solitary animals will have the hardest time adjusting to colony life and this can lead to excessive fighting. To keep fighting to a minimum, make sure that you:

- *Give the Rabbits Lots of Space.* Use the average of 20sq. ft. per rabbit as your guide. The more space rabbits have to spread out, the less likely they are to fight.
- *Entertain the Rabbits.* Bored rabbits are more likely to start fights. Providing the colony some form of entertainment (tunnels intended for cats, or levels for jumping and exploring) will help to keep tempers even.
- *Reduce Competition for Resources.* Have enough food and water available for the rabbits. Competition for resources can lead to fighting as well. Large colonies will need multiple hay bins, feed, and water dishes.
- *Separate Bucks and Does.* Left to their own devices, a colony can grow exceptionally fast. A doe is typically pregnant for a month and can conceive again immediately after giving birth. To prevent a population explosion, it will be wise to keep does and bucks in two separate colonies.

- *Provide Adequate Shelter.* Housing for the rabbits to hide in if they feel the need for privacy and a roof to protect your animals from the elements are necessary. When the rabbits' privacy and protection needs are met, they are less prone to fighting.

Breeders need to decide if solid or dirt flooring is a suitable option. Some breeders use a shed or barn for colony raising. These solid structures allow the rabbits enough space to roam while protecting them from all sides. Solid floors make for easy cleanup and prevent digging. Other breeders prefer dirt flooring. To prevent rabbits from escaping the pen, they dig fencing down into the ground around the premises. A foot should be enough to prevent escapes. Pens with dirt floors give rabbits the freedom to burl–which they love. Dirt flooring comes with an increased risk of exposure to fleas, mites, and parasites. Cleanup can be a bit more challenging, but it is possible to litter train rabbits. Whether you prefer solid or dirt floors, the main walls penning the colony should prevent rodents and predators from getting in. Solid walls or small gauge wire are commonly used.

TRACTOR RAISING

An economical solution for many homesteaders is tractor raising their rabbits. Chickens can and are successfully kept in mobile tractors. This allows the birds to remain safely confined while reducing feed costs. The same holds true for rabbits, but they'll need a fully enclosed housing unit to prevent escapes. Rabbits have an instinctual need to burrow and will dig themselves out of any confinement they are in, that's why the floor of your rabbit tractor needs the wire. The spacing has to be large enough to allow the animal to graze, but small enough to prevent escapes. Pay close attention to the wire that makes up the walls and ceiling of the tractor. Rabbits can easily chew through thin chicken wire. If you plan on using the tractor to raise litters, it's best to double-check the spacing in the wire. Those kits can squirm through the tiniest holes.

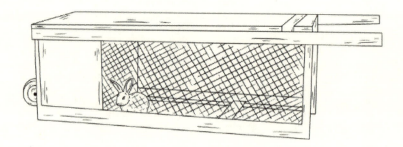

Benefits of Rabbit Tractors

Rabbit tractors can help drastically cut down on the amount of feed the animals will need. Other benefits include.

- Fresh air and sunshine for rabbits.
- Protection from small predators (foxes, weasels, and raccoons).
- Rabbits develop better muscle tone and have space to run and play.
- It becomes easier to care for multiple rabbits at a time and reduces cleanup.
- Rabbits have access to fresh food and can reduce the frequency that the grass needs to be mowed.
- Tractor raising is suitable for smaller operations and homesteads.
- Effective rabbit tractors can be made quite cheaply.

Drawbacks of Tractors

You'll need a minimum of two tractors to keep does and bucks separate, more if you plan on raising multiple litters at once. This means the number of rabbit tractors can quickly add up. Other drawbacks include.

- Tractors need to be moved daily, twice a day in most cases, to prevent rabbits from scalping the grass.
- Rabbits may be exposed to ear mites or parasites.
- Adequate shelter will need to be provided to keep rabbits protected from exposure. High temperatures can lead to rabbits overheating.
- Tractor raising is not suitable for wet or muddy conditions and can't be used in the winter in areas that are prone to snow and ice.
- This method makes it hard to collect manure.
- Tractor design needs to be light enough to remain moveable, but strong enough to keep small predators out.

RABBIT RUNS

In their natural habitat, rabbits are active creatures that keep themselves busy with running, hopping, and binkying. The latter happens when rabbits leap in the air when excited. Rabbit runs may prove to be suitable alternatives for breeders who want to keep their animals protected, but still want to afford them enough space to run and play. How much space? It is recommended that a pair of average-sized rabbits should have a run of at least 10ft. long and 6ft. wide. Typically, runs are 3ft. high, but larger breeds may need more space. The run should be high enough to allow the rabbits to freely stand on their hind legs to scout for danger.

Rabbits need access to their run at all times. The basic setup usually consists of an exercise run that is permanently connected to suitable housing, like a hutch. Just like with colony raising, some breeders prefer dirt floors while others opt for solid flooring. If you have the resources, an outdoor shed can easily be converted.

Benefits of Rabbit Runs

Active rabbits are healthy, happy animals. Rabbit runs give rabbits the freedom to run and play whilst remaining protected. Other benefits include.

- *Rabbit Runs are a Flexible Setup.* It is suitable for use indoors and outdoors. Outdoor runs with dirt floors can easily be given solid flooring by placing paving slabs on the ground. As long as the rabbit's main sleeping area and the run is connected, you've got the freedom to design the enclosure to work with the space you have available.
- *Keeps Animals Calm and Happy.* Rabbits are prey animals, so they naturally have very sensitive fight-or-flight instincts: this can put them in a stressed state very easily. By giving

them enough room to run around, breeders can prevent their rabbits from experiencing too much daily stress.

- *Encourages Healthy Development.* For young rabbits, exercise helps to strengthen their bones. The high-impact and high-intensity nature of their running, leaping, and rapid turns are necessary for them to develop into healthy adults. Runs provide the space that fryers need to grow into strong rabbits.
- *Encourage Grazing.* Runs can be placed over grass for grazing which keeps the rabbit's gut healthy. "Grazing trays" (trays planted with turf) can be added to runs that have solid flooring.

Drawbacks of Runs

Maintenance should be done carefully. Gnawing is an instinct for rabbits and it can be difficult to deter them from chewing on the run. Make sure to use untreated wood if you are constructing the run from scratch. Regular maintenance checks will help to highlight any potential weak areas of the run. Other drawbacks of rabbit runs include.

- Foxes, stoats, and weasels can pose a real danger to rabbits and can break into rabbit runs that are made from weak materials (like chicken wire). The holes in the wire should be narrow enough to prevent weasels and smaller animals from getting through.
- All doors will need to be fastened securely. Some predators can slip bolts back, which can spell disaster for your rabbits. It is best to secure doors with a sturdy padlock.
- Runs may not be suitable for use in urban areas, or if limited space is available.
- Rabbits might dig out of runs that have dirt floors. To prevent this, breeders should move the run regularly or fit a mesh skirt. Some breeders opt for fully enclosed runs by sinking mesh under the ground. If you prefer to give your rabbits the freedom to dig and you will need to maintain rabbit runs several times a week.
- Risk of parasite, mite, and flea exposure increases.

Considerations For Rabbit Runs

After choosing the size and location of your rabbit run, you'll need to consider what to put in it. Rabbits won't find an empty run appealing, so there are a few elements that need to be included:

- **Vantage Points:** As prey animals, rabbits instinctively scan for predators. In their natural environment, the ground is not level. There are higher areas that rabbits use as vantage points. We can simulate this by placing wooden platforms, blocks, boxes, and ramps in the run.
- **Tunnels:** In nature, we'll find that rabbits live in burrows. Consider using tunnels in the design of the rabbit run if applicable. Some breeders link different areas of the run with suitable tunnels, while others give their rabbits tunnels to play in. How you add tunnels to the rabbit run is up to you, but they make for a great way to keep rabbits calm and content.
- **Ample Hiding Spots:** Hiding places make rabbits feel safe. Hiding places can be as simple as a wooden box, but it will need more than one entrance or exit to prevent the animals from feeling trapped.
- **Digging And Grazing Trays:** If the run has solid flooring, digging and grazing trays are a great way to address their instincts. Digging trays can be as simple as filling a large wooden box with straw. You'll need to check regularly on these

trays, though. Rabbits can turn digging trays into litter boxes sometimes.

- **Stimulation:** Bored rabbits are more prone to fighting. Toys can be a great solution to liven up the run and cure their boredom.

Rabbits in the wild will spend most of their day foraging, so breeders try to set up their runs to encourage foraging. There are some simple ways you can encourage the behavior. For example, using a treat ball and scattering food in the enclosure can help keep rabbits stimulated. Hay should be freely available and makes for effective rabbit entertainment as well.

KINDLING BOXES

Kindling boxes (nest boxes) are placed in our does' cages a few days before they are due. There are different types of kindling boxes ranging from commercially produced metal and wooden boxes to disposable liners for built-in and sunken kindling boxes. There are advantages and drawbacks to each option.

Counterset Nest Boxes

This type of box is recessed below the hutch floor. These nest boxes can be fitted like drawers to allow easy access to the kits from outside the hutch. These nest boxes aim to simulate a more natural environment for rabbits since they are burrowing animals. With standard nest boxes, young kits can easily jump out of the box, but struggle to get back in. This can divide the litter, which means some of the kits will go hungry. The doe will only nurse one group of kits and won't return any lost rabbits to the nest.

Counterset nest boxes are easy to keep clean because the inner drawers can be removed for washing and disinfecting.

Standard Nest Boxes

Most does choose a corner in which to kindle, scratch, and gather grass. In many cases, the standard nest box would be a practical option, because it can be moved to the doe's corner of choice. Straw, (not hay) or trimmings of soft grass can be used as nesting material, but many breeders tout shredded newspaper as the ideal nesting material (Humanity Development Library 2.0, n.d.). Shredded newspapers tend to be free from canker- and mange-causing insects and mites.

When positioning the nesting box, make sure it rests at a slight angle. Some breeders tilt it at the font with a wedge of wood. This is a necessary step to protect kits from possible injury when the doe enters or exits the box. The bottom of the box should have drainage holes or mesh to keep the nest dry.

DIY Wood Nest Box

Effective nest boxes can be built at home with relatively few materials. When building a nest box, keep in mind that the sides should be at least six inches high to prevent nursing kits from being dragged out of the nest. The box needs to be heavy enough to prevent the doe from moving or tipping it. Some breeders add a wooden shelf on top of the box. The idea is to give the doe space where she can escape from pesky kits when they venture from the nest.

Nest Box Hygiene

All nest boxes should be washed and disinfected 30 days after each doe had her litter. Commercial disinfectants are available for this purpose, but if you find yourself in a pinch, a boiling saltwater solution (one cup of salt in four cups of water) can help. Simply pour the boiling saltwater onto a cleaned nest box and allow it to dry in the sun. Burning newspaper or cogon grass inside the nest box can help to sanitize it as well.

A SIMPLE RABBIT SYSTEM

A lot goes into caring for rabbits and there may be things that new breeders don't consider straight off the bat. A simple rabbit system, irrespective of the type of enclosure used, will keep the feeding area and bathroom areas at opposite ends of the hutch, pen, or run (Mitchell, 2018). The middle area is reserved for play and sleep. When setting up your rabbit system, keep in mind that space is important. You'll want to provide rabbits with enough space for a few good hops between the different areas. With a little planning, it is possible to create a rabbit system that stimulates the animals and keeps them safe from predators and the elements.

While due consideration should be given to the rabbit enclosure, we need to consider their food and water dishes, nesting boxes, resting boards, and how to keep predators away for a simple and efficient rabbit system.

Water Sources

Water shortages can lead to a multitude of problems in rabbit health. If a rabbit does not have access to adequate water, it won't eat as readily. In some cases, this can lead to starvation, sickness, and death. This is completely preventable by ensuring your rabbits have plenty of fresh water available whenever they need it. Rabbits aren't particular about using water bowls or bottles. As long as the water is fresh, available, and the animals are reacting to the source in a positive way, you are good to go.

Water Bowls

Commonly referred to as a "crock". These bowls are made of ceramic, metal, or plastic. If you settle for this option, make sure that you purchase a crock that clips to the cage, change the water twice a day, and clean the crock regularly to keep rabbits healthy and happy. If you don't have a crock that clips to the cage, try placing the water bowl in an elevated spot away from hay and bedding.

Benefits of Crocks

Wild rabbits drink their water from ground sources, so a crock provides a natural way for them to drink water. Other benefits include.

- Crocks are fairly easy to clean and refill.
- Replacing broken crocks is inexpensive.
- Breeders who keep rabbits outside during winter will find that crocks are less prone to breakage when the water freezes over.

Drawbacks of Crocks

While crocks provide a natural way for rabbits to drink, there are some drawbacks. Water tends to evaporate more readily in a crock than in a bottle, which means it'll need regular refilling, especially during the hot summer months. Other potential drawbacks include.

- Water bowls can quickly become contaminated with hay, bedding, and urine and will need regular cleaning.
- During the summer, crocks can collect bugs or begin to grow algae.
- Rabbits commonly tip over and play with their water bowl, especially when it is not secured.
- Rabbits will gnaw on plastic water dishes.
- May not be a suitable option for breeders who don't have a lot of spare time. Breeders may need to check on water bowls multiple times a day to ensure enough clean water is available.
- Crocks are not suitable for use when liquid medications need to be administered.

Water/Medicine Bottle

Water bottles are a cleaner option, as rabbits can't soil this water source with hay and other contaminants.

These bottles often prove to be an easier option, but nothing is without flaws.

Benefits of Bottles

Water bottles tend to be a low-maintenance option that easily negates some of the glaring drawbacks that crocks present.

- Water bottles give rabbits a reliable source of clean water.
- There's less wasting of water since rabbits can't tip, contaminate or play with their water source.
- Helps to free up time for the breeder as they will spend less time checking, cleaning, and refilling water sources.
- Can be used to administer water-soluble medications.

Drawbacks of Bottles

Rabbits may find water bottles awkward to use. Drinking from a bottle is not a natural behavior for these animals and having their neck tilted to drink may cause damage in later years if the bottle is placed at an incorrect height (Rabbit Hole Hay, 2019). Water bottles should be placed high enough to allow the rabbits to keep their necks straight while drinking. Other draw-backs include.

- Less accessible water for rabbits. Water bottle feeders only let rabbits drink little bits at a time, which can become tedious, especially for thirsty rabbits. This means that rabbits spend more time trying to drink with their head in an awkward position.
- Due to the slow water delivery method, breeders will need several water bottles to keep rabbits hydrated.
- Thirsty rabbits will crowd around a water bottle, increasing competition for water which can lead to fighting, stress, and poor health in the animals.
- Bottles can clog. The ball can get stuck and the spout can clog fairly easily. This is usually the result of a buildup of residue as rabbits go back and forth between eating and drinking.

Food Dishes and Dispensers

What will your rabbits eat and how will they be eating it? In the wild, rabbits will spend hours grazing on grass, shoots, and leaves. The way breeders provide their rabbits with food can have a big impact on their well-being (Stone, n.d.). Food can be used to encourage foraging as well as to keep rabbits calm and content. There are a few options for presenting rabbits with food. We'll take a look at each in turn.

Food Bowls

This classic option is commonly made from heavy-duty plastic, metal, or ceramic. For hutches with more than one level, it may be best to use a dish that can be attached to the cage. A coop cup will work well in most cases, especially if the rabbits are prone to eliminate in their bowls. They are inexpensive and have many of the same benefits and drawbacks as water bowls. These bowls are easy to clean and refill, but rabbits can tip them over if they are not secured. Keep in mind that rabbits only need a limited number of pellets and most rabbit food dishes hold several times the amount that a rabbit would need. One crucial downside that breeders need to keep in mind is that food bowls can discourage foraging. It makes everything very easy for the rabbit since the food can be effortlessly obtained.

Food Ball

Breeders who want to encourage foraging behavior while providing their rabbits with some mental stimulation often make use of food balls (treat balls). These encourage rabbits to work for their food as they nudge and manipulate the hollow treat ball to obtain food.

Treat balls doubles up as a toy, but may prove insufficient for large-scale breeding. Also, some treat balls have knobby plastic bits that rabbits can chew off.

Fresh Food Bowl Options

There are a variety of creative alternatives when presenting fresh food to rabbits. Some breeders use a hanging wire basket that is filled with fresh food, whilst others prefer a metal skewer to thread vegetable chunks on. By adjusting the height of the wire basket or metal skewer, rabbits are encouraged to stretch and work for their food. When using metal skewers in this manner, make sure that they have screw ends to keep the vegetables in place.

Scatter Feeding

This option encourages rabbits to forage and eliminates the need to clean up food dishes. Breeders simply scatter the food in the rabbit enclosure. This method is used when rabbits display food-related aggression, but it may not be a suitable feeding method for hutch enclosures.

Resting Boards

Resting boards provide a space for rabbits to rest their feet away from the wire flooring of their enclosure. Various options are available ranging from ceramic tiles and untreated wood boards to commercially produced plastic resting boards with drainage holes. Whichever option the breeder goes for, they need to ensure the board is easy to clean and made from rabbit-friendly materials. If your rabbits are gnawers, it is best to steer clear of plastic resting boards.

KEEPING PREDATORS AWAY

Rabbits are prey animals, so it is not surprising that local predators may deem them as a tasty and easily accessible snack. Hawks, foxes, and other predators can wreak havoc in a vulnerable rabbit enclosure, undoing all the hard work you've put in towards raising them.

Predators don't differentiate between a domesticated rabbit and a wild one. They are animals of opportunity. To them, food is food, and rabbits living outside are easy targets. Predators are not the only threat to rabbits. Some domesticated animals may hunt and kill rabbits. Some predators hunt during the daytime, while others hunt at night. The most common predators to protect rabbits from include:

- *Foxes:* These animals hunt at night and sleep during the day.
- *Felines:* Pet cats, bobcats, and other small wild cats will hunt at any time of the day.

- *Canines:* Domestic dogs, wolves, and coyotes are opportunistic feeders and will hunt whenever the opportunity presents itself.
- *Badgers and Raccoons:* These animals are nocturnal and will wreak havoc in a rabbit enclosure at night. Those cute little trash pandas (raccoons) have another trick up their sleeve: they can manipulate and pull back bolts that are not secured, which can lead to an extensive loss for the breeder.
- *Birds of Prey:* Hawks, falcons, kestrels, and owls will hunt rabbits at different times of the day.
- *Stoats and Weasels:* These animals are nocturnal during the winter months, but change their habits to become diurnal in the summer. Stoats can be particularly bothersome, as they can wiggle through relatively small spaces.
- *Snake Species:* Large snakes like gopher snakes and rattlesnakes will hunt rabbits at any time of the day, depending on the species. Just like stoats, snakes can squeeze through relatively tight spaces to get into a rabbit enclosure.

Predators vary by area. Some breeders face a bigger risk from raccoons and snakes, while others need to contend with foxes. Knowing which predators can be found in your area will help you prepare a predator-proof enclosure. Some general steps breeders can take to keep predators at bay include:

- Having a dog patrolling the property. This will deter cats, foxes, raccoons, and other wild animals from entering the property.
- Keeping the rabbitry close to their homes. Predators are naturally leery of humans and will avoid contact whenever possible.
- Use night lights. This is a good deterrent for nocturnal predators as their instincts will lead them to shy away from bright night lights.
- Don't leave scraps of meat laying about in the yard, as it can lure opportunistic predators like raccoons, foxes, and dogs.
- Build enclosures high up, making it harder for predators to get into the space.
- Removing piles of hay or pellets under rabbit cages, to discourage predators from attacking the animals through the wire floors.
- Trail cameras can be used to identify what kind of predator is targeting your rabbits. Once you know what predator you are dealing with it becomes easier to protect your rabbits.
- Use electric fencing if need be.

Protecting Rabbits From Land-Based Predators

Foxes and raccoons are some of the most common predators a rabbit breeder will encounter. These animals are typically found in urban and rural areas and will hunt any creature that is small enough. Apply these tips to keep rabbits safe from land-based predators:

- *Keep Rabbits Indoors:* The most effective way to ensure the safety of your rabbits is to keep them indoors; however, this may not be a viable solution for all breeders. A large shed can be converted into a rabbitry, as long as the walls are sturdy, predators will have a hard time getting in.
- *Predator-Proof the Hutch:* Hutches made from cheap plywood or chicken wire won't hold up to the efforts of a hungry fox. Use strong materials when building a hutch and secure door latches with padlocks to keep pesky raccoons out. Rabbit runs and pens that are mass-produced typically don't have a floor or roof. Foxes can easily dig underneath or jump and climb over fences and have a field day in the enclosure. For this reason, many breeders opt to add wire flooring and roofing to their enclosures.

- *Give Rabbits Ample Hiding Spots:* Rabbits are sensitive creatures and can die from fear. While this is rare, rabbits can suffer cardiac arrest when confronted with a predator or frightening situations (such as loud noises coming from exploding fireworks). For this reason, rabbits need secluded hiding spots that they can use whenever they feel vulnerable.
- *Make Your Yard Unappealing for Predators:* A predator-proof rabbit enclosure is half the battle won. Breeders will need to actively discourage predators from entering their property by keeping their grass short, covering any standing water that could attract animals, and keeping trash cans tightly lidded. Motion-detecting lights can help to deter nocturnal predators from exploring the property.

Protecting Rabbits From Ariel Threats

If your rabbitry is fox-proof, it should be safe from birds of prey as well. However, we need to keep in mind that birds of prey are not always afraid of humans like foxes are. A hawk can easily swoop down and scoop up a rabbit in open or uncovered runs and pens, even if a human is present (Carter, 2019). To deter birds of prey, breeders ensure that the pen and run have a roof that is made from wood paneling or strong wire mesh. Other deterrents include:

- *Hanging Shiny and Reflective Objects Near the Enclosure:* Hawks and kestrels hunt from above. While their hunting method has advantages, it makes them vulnerable to reflected light. Birds of prey can become disoriented when light is reflected in their eyes, preventing them from locking on to their target and landing. An easy way to deter birds of prey is by hanging unwanted CDs in your yard.
- *Scarecrows:* These life-sized decoys can be seen in farmer's fields and are used to scare birds away from sown crops. Depending on the birds of prey found in your area, scarecrows may or may not work. Birds of prey are intelligent and not easily fooled. Some breeders use life-sized statutes of owls to deter hawks, as hawks are afraid of owls. To ensure the decoy remains effective, move it to different spots on the property every few days, otherwise, hawks and kestrels will catch on to the ruse.

Keeping Dogs Away From The Rabbitry

Some dogs, like terriers, are bred to hunt rabbits. They have strong hunting instincts and a docile rabbit makes for an easy target. To keep dogs out of the rabbit enclosure, it is best to erect a high perimeter fence, ideally made from solid panel wood. Some dogs that are determined to wreak mayhem will climb fences, so a solid panel option will prevent this. This does not solve all your dog-related problems though. Consider the following measures to keep your rabbit enclosure canine-free:

- Bury wire at the base of the fence to discourage digging.
- Ensure the rabbit enclosure is predator-proof.
- Spray undiluted vinegar around the perimeter of your property and rabbit enclosure to deter dogs. Dogs have sensitive noses and the smell of vinegar can be irritating for them. Reapply the vinegar on a daily basis to keep the scent from fading.

If you are a proud dog owner, don't let them near the rabbitry unsupervised. Train your dogs to respond to the commands of "stop," "heel" and "stay." Barking and aggression should be discouraged around rabbits.

Keeping Cats Away From The Rabbitry

Cats (domestic and wild) will hunt anything small and furry or feathered. That means birds, mice, and rabbits are fair game for a hungry cat. Cats also hunt for sport, so breeders with domestic cats will need to take additional steps to keep their rabbits safe. Some cats get along with rabbits, but we should regard this as an exception and not the rule. To keep cats in the area away from the rabbitry, try the following tips:

- *Cat-Proof Fences:* Ever spotted fences with a roller at the top? These rollers are an ingenious solution and spin whenever a cat attempts to climb over it. Sharp spikes placed along the top of the fence can also help to keep roaming cats out of an area.

- *Use Cat Repellent:* There's a good reason why you'll likely never see a cat in a citrus tree. The citrus oils irritate their delicate noses. One way that breeders can harness the power of citrus is by placing fresh orange and lemon peels on the property. Ultrasonic cat alarms can prove useful, since they emit high-frequency noise to deter feline intruders.

- *Motion-Activated Sprinklers:* Cats' hatred of water is legendary. If a cat is sprayed enough times, it'll soon avoid your property altogether. Motion-activated sprinklers can be used to effectively deter any "cat burglars" in your rabbitry.

Breeders often use a combination of techniques to keep their rabbits safe. Now that we have a better idea of how to house rabbits, new breeders will need to find the right breed. Some rabbit breeds are better suited for meat production, while others are best for wool. The next chapter will help you find the right breed.

2

THE RIGHT BREED FOR YOU

Rabbit meat is enjoyed all over the world in a variety of dishes. Rabbit meat is considered lean white meat and is low in calories and cholesterol-free (Jakob, 2020). Not all rabbits are suitable meat animals, making the selection of the correct breed is all the more important. Good meat rabbits make economic sense as they will give breeders more meat on less feed.

Quality breeding stock is worth investing in as thrifty lines will pay for themselves in feed savings. A good tip to keep in mind when purchasing rabbits is to ask for the breeder's records. A good breeder will be able to tell you what their kits weigh at eight weeks. If the breeder can't share this bit of basic information with you, it is best to look elsewhere. Beginners are advised to keep these general characteristics in mind when selecting a rabbit breed:

- The rabbits should have naturally muscular bodies.
- Meat-to-bone ratio should be higher than in other breeds. Foot size is a good indicator of this.
- Meat rabbits should be easy to maintain and possess good quality fur.
- These breeds have a quick growth rate and large body size.
- Offspring from these rabbits tend to be uniform in size and fast growers.
- When selecting rabbits with these characteristics in mind, adult rabbits would weigh between eight to 12 pounds and deliver a 60% dress-out rate on average.

It can be tempting to add large-boned rabbits, like the Flemish Giant, to the breeding stock to increase growth rates, but this is not a good idea. While breeders might be proud of their five-pound fryers at eight weeks, those fryers will eat them out of house and home before reaching a butchering weight. Keep in mind that rabbits grow bone before they plump up, so a fine bone structure is ideal.

Rabbit breeds can broadly be lumped into three categories: commercial breeds, heritage breeds, and hybrids. Each category has benefits and drawbacks. Let's take a closer look.

Commercial Breeds

New Zealand and Californian rabbits come to mind when we speak of commercial breeds. These rabbits tend to rank among the most popular breeds used for commercial production. These breeds are touted for their large litter size and considerable fast growth.

Benefits:

- Easily obtainable from many breeders.
- These rabbits tend to be fairly large.
- Can be bred for meat, pelt, and shows.
- They gain weight quickly and have a good meat-to-bone ratio.
- Suitable for breeders who have advanced past the novice stage and want to expand their rabbitry.

Drawbacks:

- Breeds with red eyes are not suited for tractor raising, because their eyes are sensitive to sunlight.

- Breeders may incur higher feed expenses with red-eyed breeds.
- It may yield a lower dress-out rate than other breeds.
- The chances of kit death increase due to large litter sizes.
- Breeders may need to foster kits in some cases.

Heritage Breeds

Heritage breeds tend to have smaller litter sizes and gentle temperaments. They tend to be better suited to backyards, small farms, and homesteaders and can easily be raised on a pasture in rabbit tractors (Alyssa, 2019).

Benefits:

- Heritage breeds are a good choice for novice breeders, as they can be raised fairly cheaply and quickly.
- Smaller litter sizes help to keep rabbit numbers manageable.
- They gain muscle mass easily and have a lower bone density.
- Tend to yield higher dress-out rates.

- Chances of kit death are reduced as the litter sizes are smaller and more manageable for the doe.
- Suitable for beginners and breeders who prefer small operations.
- These rabbits can be raised for meat and can be kept as pets.

Drawbacks:

- Due to their relatively small size, some breeders prefer to wait a few extra weeks before butchering, sacrificing efficiency for weight.
- It is harder to predator-proof rabbit enclosures housing small breeds, as they easily squirm through tight gaps.
- Their docile nature makes heritage breeds easy pickings for predators.

Hybrid Breeds

Each category of rabbit has benefits and drawbacks, but some breeders want the best of both worlds: a quick-growing, meaty rabbit with a docile temperament. With hybrid breeds, it is possible to achieve this. If you cross a commercial breed with a heritage breed, the resulting kits will likely have the fast growth rate of the former and the weight-gaining prowess of the latter.

Benefits:

- Hybrids deliver the highest dress-out rate.
- Grows fast and is efficient on feed.
- Suitable for operations that focus on strict meat production.

Drawbacks:

- Breeders will need to maintain pure commercial and heritage lines. If you start to breed the offspring of hybrids, they will soon lose the desired traits of their parents (Klein, 2019).
- Due to the scale and complexity involved with hybrids, this is considered to be expert-level rabbit raising.
- Breeders will need in-depth knowledge of the rabbits they are hybridizing to produce desirable meat rabbits.

HACKING GROWTH RATES

Meat rabbits are typically raised to 8-10 weeks of age and can weigh five pounds before processing. Smaller breeds and rabbits with non-meat genetics and feed rabbits will take a bit longer to raise. Litter size will impact the animals' growth rate. The larger the litter, the longer it will take for kits to reach the five-pound mark. Typically, a litter of 10 to 14 weaned kits can take 11 weeks to reach the desired weight, whereas a small litter (three to four kits) can be processed at eight weeks.

Breeders who want their rabbits ready for processing at the 10-week mark employ a variety of strategies, including:

- *Using Pellets With 18% Protein:* Pellet feed is formulated for optimal growth and rabbit health and can aid in the reduction of feed waste. Since these pellets are fortified with vitamins and minerals, breeders can rest assured that their animals are getting the nutrients they need to grow quickly. While 18% protein feed tends to be on the pricey and hard-to-find side, it can make a substantial difference to rabbit growth. Feeds with lower protein percentages can be used, but they result in slower growth.
- *Supplementing Sparingly With Other Feeds:* Other feeds, like hay or vegetables, lower the energy of the total food ration, resulting in slower weight gain. For this reason, many breeders treat vegetables and hay like a treat,

occasionally supplementing their rabbits' feed. Any variation in your rabbits' raising system or feed will result in slower gains and is something breeders should keep in mind.

- *Avoiding Forage-Based Diets:* If a quick raising cycle is vital to the breeder, they might opt to avoid forage-based diets altogether. This does not mean grass-fed rabbits can't reach butchering weight! Not at all. Grass-fed rabbits and those raised pens will take a little longer to reach the desired weight, simply because they are burning off more energy. If a breeder has their heart set on grass-fed rabbits, go for it! Just be aware that the raising time is longer. If the breeder wants fast-growing rabbits, they'll need to stay in a hutch or pen and feed on 18% pellets for optimal results.

Troubleshooting Slow-Growing Rabbits

There's no escaping the fact that achieving five-pound fryers at the 10-week mark requires high-quality breeding stock. One of the biggest reasons rabbits may take longer to raise lies in genetics. Remember, meat rabbits have the genes for fast growth so good genetics will pay off by providing breeders with economical gains (savings on feed and quick growth time). Keep in mind that all breeds have high-performers and poor performers, so select your breeding stock carefully. While genetics play a dominant role, two other factors can influence rabbit growth.

- *Lack of Water:* Restrict water and you restrict growth. It is as simple as that. The biggest culprit? Over-reliance on water bottles and neglecting crocks. Breeders who use water bottles exclusively as their rabbits' water source are inadvertently restricting growth. Rabbits consume up to three times more water out of an open crock than out of a water bottle (Mccune, 2022). This is no big surprise, as crocks make for easy drinking. Rabbits have a habit of contaminating crocks and messing with water, which also restricts the availability of water. The best solution is to supply rabbits with water bottles and crocks. That way, if the crock becomes soiled, the rabbits still have a clean source of water. Fast-growing animals need unfettered access to water to process their food.
- *Discomfort:* Rabbits are sensitive animals and will need to be kept in comfortable conditions for optimal growth. To get the most out of your rabbits, keep their enclosure clean, give the litter plenty of room, have ample fresh water

available, and protect them from heat. Rabbits are comfortable in temperatures averaging 65 degrees, so make sure to shade them or use fans if needed. All of these steps are aimed at stress reduction. Stressed animals won't grow or process their food optimally.

The guideline below will help breeders determine if their commercial breeds are growing optimally. It is advised that serious breeders obtain a copy of the Standard of Perfection for their selected breeds.

Age	Average Weight in Pounds	Excellent Growth Weight
Six Weeks	2.7 lbs.	3 lbs. and above
Eight Weeks	4 lbs.	4.25 lbs. and above
10 Weeks	5 lbs.	5.5 lbs. and above
12 Weeks	6 lbs.	6.5 lbs. and above

PURCHASING YOUR FIRST RABBIT

A big mistake novices make when purchasing their first rabbits is going to the pet store. These rabbits are products of mass-breeding facilities that can be likened to puppy mills. So, it is safe to say that good meat genetics is not a priority. Besides, pet rabbits and meat rabbits have significantly different growth rates. A budding breeder might turn to online sources and auctions next, but there is no guarantee of quality or fair pricing here. Rabbits adopted from shelters are suitable pets, but make for poor breeding stock. If you take your rabbit raising seriously, your best option is to purchase your first long ears from a reputable breeder.

Identifying a Reputable Breeder

Good rabbit breeders are not in the business just for some greenbacks. One of the hallmarks of a good and responsible breeder is their personal involvement in each sale and their refusal to sell animals to a pet store or third parties. Good rabbit breeders can be found by contacting local breed clubs, visiting rabbit shows, or asking for references from trusted people and veterinarians. You should always visit the breeder before purchasing any animals. While you are visiting, keep an eye out for the following:

- *Condition of the Rabbits:* The rabbits should look healthy and happy and be housed in clean, well-maintained, and well-lit enclosures.
- *Veterinary Records:* Responsible breeders have a good relationship with their local vet and should be able to provide records and references on the care of their rabbits.
- *Knowledge and Interest:* The breeder should explain common genetic problems that occur in

your selected breeds. Furthermore, the breeder should be able to provide references to other individuals who have purchased from them. Breeders that have the best interests of their rabbits at heart will encourage buyers to read and sign a written contract with a health guarantee, requiring that buyers visit a predetermined vet (The Humane Society of the United States, 2022). Good breeders tend to be involved in local, state, or national breeding clubs and will ask buyers what their experiences with rabbits are. These breeders may even ask for a veterinary reference.

Ultimately, it is best to choose a breeder who has cared well for their animals and can provide buyers with records on how much their fryers weigh at eight weeks of age. If a breeder cannot provide these records or is hesitant, it is best to take your search elsewhere. Try to find rabbits with a pedigree. This will help to offset the costs of feed. Pedigreed rabbits will sell much faster and will fetch a better price than regular rabbits.

When bringing new rabbits home, it is necessary to quarantine the animals for two weeks away from the other animals. This necessary step will help you determine if the animal is healthy and will prevent healthy animals from getting sick, see First Aid and Disease Prevention for more details.

This Is My First Time Raising Rabbits. How Old Should My First Breeding Pair Be?

One-year-old adult rabbits are often the easiest to handle when you are new to rabbit raising. Young rabbits tend to be rambunctious and will frequently chew and dig as they explore their environment. Year-old rabbits are easier to litter train and can be bred, resulting in a rabbitry that is productive from the start, which is a big help when you are learning the ropes. Consider the size and purpose of the rabbit as well. Smaller breeds tend to be very active and can be skittish at times, while larger breeds tend to be easygoing.

BEST MEAT BREEDS

The American Rabbit Breeders Association recognizes 49 rabbit breeds (Hall, n.d.). When hunting for a breed, it is recommended to look at what breeds are available locally. These rabbits would have had generations to adapt to the local climate, making them good options for homesteaders. Breeders are encouraged to make sure that their selected rabbit breed will be comfortable in their local climate. Silver Foxes might struggle in warm areas due to their thick coat, whereas black rabbits will need extra sun protection.

It is a good idea to find a breed that is fairly common locally, but not too common. You'll have a hard time selling your rabbits if all the local breeders have the same rabbit breeds you do. In the same vein, if you end up being the sole breeder of an exotic rabbit breed, you may have trouble purchasing new stock. Therefore, breed selection merits careful consideration. Many breeders agree that mid-sized breeds like the New Zealand White and California are great choices for homesteaders (Rise and Shine Rabbitry, 2012).

New Zealand

This popular breed comes in a variety of colors, including red, although white is the most popular. These rabbits have chubby cheeks and a sweet, affectionate nature. The breed's name is a bit misleading, as it was developed in the USA for fur, meat and exhibition purposes. These rabbits are a commercial breed that tends to be slender and muscular. Their smallish, wedge-shaped faces and stumpy muzzles are easily recognizable and their ears will stand erect and be of medium length. These rabbits have dense, luxurious coats and the kits mature quickly. Other reasons to consider the New Zealand include:

- Mature rabbits weigh between 9 and 12 pounds. Does average a weight of 10 to 12 pounds, while bucks weigh 10 to 11 pounds.
- Does are good mothers and the average litter size ranges between 7 and 14 kits.
- These rabbits can be kept as pets or raised for fur and meat.
- The breed has soft flyback fur that does not require extra grooming.
- Good indoor and outdoor rabbits.
- The breed has an average lifespan of five to eight years.
- Suitable for novice breeders.
- The breed is not listed by the American Livestock Conservancy (ALC) and four color varieties are recognized by the American Rabbit Breeders Association (Irvine, 2019b).

Drawbacks of The Breed:

- Does can become a bit testy and protective after kindling.
- New Zealands can become moody during mating season.

Californian

The Californian is a breed that loves to play, but they can be timid at times. This commercial breed is easily recognizable by its short ears that are rounded at the tips and positioned close together on the head. Californians have well-muscled bodies with coarse, dense coats. Other reasons to consider the breed include:

- Can be bred for meat, fur, shows, and kept as pets.
- This is a large breed. Does average a weight of 12 pounds and bucks 10 pounds.
- The average lifespan of the breed ranges from 5–10 years.
- The Californian has a gentle temperament and is suitable for novice breeders.
- Does make good mothers and the kits grow at a good rate.
- Litter sizes range from 8–12 kits.
- Can easily be kept in all climates.

Drawbacks of The Breed:

- Californians will need a bigger enclosure that allows them to run and expend their energies.

- Can develop sore hocks and is best housed in enclosures that have solid flooring or have ample rest boards available.
- Will need regular health checkups and are prone to fly-strike if kept outside (Irvine, 2019f).
- The American Rabbit Breeders Association recognizes only one-color variation.
- Very active and curious breed that will need stimulation from their environment. This includes toys, tunnels, and platforms that the rabbits can interact and play with.
- Pelt is not as desirable as other breeds due to its coarse nature.

Palomino

This heritage breed was developed in the USA. The Palomino is a large, hardy breed that is recognizable by its orange coloring and white undercoat, although other color variations exist. They have a docile, sweet temperament. Other reasons to consider Palomino include:

- Palominos have a small bone structure, making them excellent meat rabbits with an excellent meat-to-bone ratio.

- Does make good mothers and litter sizes range from four to 12 kits.
- Both sexes average at 8–12 pounds at maturity (Irvine, 2019d).
- Enjoy human company and make for sought-after pets and exhibition rabbits.
- Their short, medium rollback fur does not require special grooming.
- The breed is not listed by the ALC and the American Rabbit Breeders Association recognizes two color varieties.
- This breed can be safely raised in all climates.

Drawbacks of The Breed:

- Due to their large size, the Palomino breed needs a large enclosure to remain healthy.
- Rabbits take a little longer to mature than other breeds.

Satin

This popular medium to large breed comes in a variety of colors. These rabbits are hardy, well-mannered creatures sporting a well-rounded body shape. Their reddish-brown eyes and silky coat make them attractive exhibition breeds. Other reasons breeders choose the Satin include:

- Sought after exhibition and pet breed. Satins are usually well-received at rabbit shows, which provides another possible income source for the breeder.
- Coats are dense, soft, and prized which creates another possibility of generating income.
- Both sexes weigh 8–12 pounds on maturity.
- Can be kept indoors or outdoors.
- Can be kept in all climates.
- Not listed by the ALC. The American Rabbit Breeders Association recognizes 11 coat colors of this breed.

Drawbacks of The Breed:

- Litter size varies from one kit to a dozen (Irvine, 2019i). The kits tend to mature on the slower side, reducing the overall production efficiency of this breed.
- Will need a large enclosure to remain healthy.

Champagne D'Argent

D'Argent in French means silver or silvery—beautifully describing this breed's coat color. Some believe the breed dates back to the mid-1600s and there are quite a few D'Argent rabbit breeds, although only a few are recognized by the American Rabbit Breeders Association. These gorgeous rabbits have an equally beautiful temperament, making them a sought-after breed. Other reasons breeders prefer the Champagne include:

- Champagnes are large, multipurpose breeds. They can be kept for meat, exhibitions, pets and fur.
- Does weigh 12 pounds on average while bucks average 9.4 pounds.
- Does make good mothers and litters are moderately sized, ranging between five and eight kits.

- Average lifespan ranges from seven to nine years.
- Can be successfully kept in all climates.
- The breed is not listed by the ALC and is recognized by the American Rabbit Breeders Association.
- Good meat rabbit with a wide midsection. The loin is deep and the breed yields a good meat-to-bone ratio.
- The breed is known to have a fine bone structure and reaches slaughter weight in under 90 days.

Drawbacks of The Breed:

- Does may become a bit aggressive during the mating season and when they have kits (Irvine, 2019g).
- Due to their dark coat color, these rabbits will need extra protection from the sun.
- Very sociable animals and will need toys and other sources of stimulation in their enclosures.
- This breed will need a large enclosure to remain healthy.

American Chinchilla

This beautiful rabbit is the rarest of the Chinchilla breeds and was once very popular. These large rabbits are easily recognizable by their soft salt-and-pepper fur, large erect ears, and round faces. Benefits of the breed include:

- Does make good mothers and have litter ranging from 8–10 kits.
- Makes great meat rabbits and produces quality meat. The breed has a good meat-to-bone ratio with a deep loin and broad shoulders.
- The breed is large with does averaging 10–12 pounds and bucks ranging from 9 to 11 pounds.
- American Chinchillas generally live five to eight years and are a hardy, low-maintenance breed with a good temperament.
- Multipurpose breed and is suitable for meat, show, and pet endeavors.
- Fryers quickly grow to a marketable size.
- Can be successfully raised in all climates and is recognized by the American Rabbit Breeders Association.
- Produces a desirable pelt.

Drawbacks of The Breed:

- The breed is rare, making it challenging for breeders to acquire new breeding stock. The rarity of the breed also means these rabbits will be pricier.
- Listed by the ALC as critically endangered (Irvine, 2019a). These rabbits were bred for meat and fur purposes, but the decline of the fur trade triggered the decline in their numbers.

Rex

This large commercial breed earned its reputation as the "king of rabbit breeds" due to its fur and meat-production abilities. The breed sports a plush, velvety coat and makes for a good exhibition animal. Other reasons to consider the Rex include:

- Rabbits have a calm, gentle nature making them sought-after pets. They've been known to actively seek attention from their human handlers.
- Does average a weight of 10.5 pounds while males reach a weight of 9.5 pounds (Irvine, 2019c).
- Coats are low-maintenance and do not require special grooming.

- The average lifespan ranges between five and eight years.
- Can be raised in all climates.
- The breed is not listed by the ALC and the American Rabbit Breeders Association recognizes 16 varieties.
- Litter size is moderate, ranging between six and eight kits.
- Easy to handle and not as jumpy as other breeds, making the breed beginner-friendly.
- Multipurpose rabbits are raised for meat, and fur and can serve as companion animals.

Drawbacks of The Breed:

- Due to its large size, the Rex rabbit will need a large enclosure to remain active and healthy.
- Bucks can become aggressive when they reach mating age.
- While these rabbits are described as boisterous and playful, they can become nippy.

Silver Fox

This heritage breed is the result of selective cross-breeding and was developed in America. Sometimes the breed is confused with the Silver Marten, but there is a noticeable difference between the two. The Silver Fox has longer hair that remains upright when brushed back to front and sports silver tips. The Silver Marten has solid coloring with silver-tipped guard hairs on the belly, sides, and rump. There are many reasons to choose this standout breed, including:

- This breed has a high dress-out ratio and it is possible to achieve a 65% dress-out ratio (Irvine, 2019e).
- Does have wonderful maternal instincts and will foster orphaned kits.
- Multipurpose breed kept for meat, fur, shows, and as pets.
- Can be raised in all climates.
- The breed is recognized by the American Rabbit Breeders Association.
- These rabbits have an average lifespan of five to eight years.
- The breed is known to have a good temperament.
- A good homestead rabbit that weighs between 9 and 12 pounds. Kits grow out fairly quickly. Does average between 10 and 12 pounds while bucks tip the scales at 9–12 pounds.
- Litters are moderately sized, varying from six kits to a dozen.

Drawbacks of The Breed:

- Listed by the ALC as a rare breed.
- Large rabbits need a large enclosure to remain happy and healthy.

Florida White

This medium-sized breed is known for its perfect white coat and red eyes. The Florida White has a docile temperament, making them excellent multi-purpose rabbits that breeders keep for meat, shows, fur, and as companion animals. Other reasons breeders prefer this breed includes:

- Small bone structure translates into a good meat-to-bone ratio, making Florida Whites a good meat rabbit. The breed dresses out very well and delivers good quality meat.
- Bucks and does average a weight of five pounds when mature.
- Coats do not need extra grooming and the rabbits have an average lifespan of five to eight years.
- The breed is not listed by the ALC and is recognized by the American Rabbit Breeders Association (Irvine, 2019h).
- Can be successfully raised in all climates.

- There is not a lot of variation in physical characteristics between individuals, making the breed suitable for commercial purposes.
- Litter sizes are moderate, ranging from six to eight kits.
- Florida Whites do not shed very much when compared to other breeds, making them desirable companion animals.

Drawbacks of The Breed:

- Red-eyed rabbits require extra sun protection and may not be suitable for tractor raising.

When selecting a breed, try not to be drawn in by breed hype. Each breed has its merits and drawbacks that need to be carefully weighed and measured against what is practical for the aspiring breeder. Large breeds might deliver more meat, but they tend to eat more and need more space to remain healthy. Smaller breeds are more accommodating if limited space is an issue, but may not deliver the desired quantity of meat a breeder may want. Therefore, breeders are encouraged to research their chosen breeds carefully. Once you have settled on a breed, hop on to the next chapter where you'll learn about the correct care and handling of rabbits.

3

RABBIT CARE 101: HANDLING, DIET, AND NUTRITION

HANDLING RABBITS THE RIGHT WAY

Rabbits have strong, muscular hind legs and delicate skeletons, increasing the risk of breaking their backs. If their bodies are not fully supported, especially the hind legs, their backs can sustain an injury or break if the rabbit decides to kick. For this reason, rabbits should never be picked up by the ears or pinned on their backs. The steps below will help prevent injury to the rabbit:

- ***Step One:*** Hold the rabbit still by grasping the scruff firmly. The scruff is the loose skin located over the rabbit's shoulders.

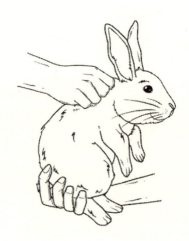

- **Step Two:** Place one hand under the rabbit's front armpits. Release the scruff and place your free hand on the rabbit's rump, close to the hind leg.

- **Step Three:** Lift the rabbit and hold it securely to your body. Support the rabbit's back at all times.

Shy Rabbits prefer to have their eyes covered. This method will also calm a struggling rabbit.

It is advisable to practice handling rabbits close to the floor. That way, injury can be prevented if the rabbit suddenly leaps. Keep in mind that rabbits don't naturally like being picked up. They'll need to be trained to trust you and allow you to handle them. Rabbits can scratch. It is best to wear long sleeves and gloves when moving and handling rabbits if you can't clip their toenails regularly.

Fixing Aggressive Behavior

Rabbits can be trained to stop aggressive behavior as follows: pin the rabbit gently but firmly by pressing down on its back. This lets the rabbit know you are the boss. Next, you'll need to cover the rabbit's eyes to calm them and tuck them right away in your armpit, holding the rabbit close. If you are going to place the rabbit in a carrier, or need to walk with it, do so immediately. Breeders must handle and pet all of their rabbits regularly so they can become accustomed to the breeder's scent and feel safe around them.

Rabbits may bite, especially during mating season or if a doe is with her kits. Never react or swat the animals when this happens. You want the rabbits to associate your hands and scent with that of kindness.

In some cases, spaying can help to control aggression in bucks. Bucks tend to become aggressive from 8 to 18 months of age, depending on the breed. This usually goes hand in hand with territory marking. When rabbits are kept as pets, spaying can help to control and prevent aggression issues in bucks, but only if the procedure was done early enough.

Litter Box Training Rabbits

Rabbits can be trained to use a litter box very easily. When training the rabbit, restrict it to a small area. Next, you'll want to place a litter box in the corner that that rabbit prefers to eliminate in. The sides of the box should be low, making it easy for the rabbit to get and out. Some breeders place droppings and some hay inside the litter box to encourage rabbits to use it. This makes sense, as rabbits tend to pass stool when eating.

Quantity And Bedding

A rule of thumb is to place one more litter box in the enclosure than the number of rabbits it houses. In an enclosure housing five does, six litter boxes will need to be available.

Non-toxic pelleted litter is the best bedding to use if odors are a concern. The litter is digestible, so it poses no risk to the rabbits if eaten, and it draws moisture away from the surface to control odor. Alternatively, the box can be lined with some hay, but it will need a regular cleanup. Never use clay or clumping kitty litter —they can cause potentially fatal blockages in the animal's intestines.

Rabbit Handling FAQ

Many new rabbit owners underestimate the level of care these animals need to stay healthy and prevent costly veterinary bills. The upside is, that once you have a fair understanding of their unique anatomy and dietary needs, caring for them becomes a lot easier.

How Do Rabbits Differ From Other Domestic Animals?

Domestic animals like cats and dogs are predators, while rabbits are prey animals. This means there will be a difference in how these animals behave when sick. It's generally easy to see when a cat or dog is ill, but rabbits are tricky because they hide their signs of illness. Rabbits like a quiet environment, whilst cats and dogs don't mind noise to a certain degree. Also, rabbits don't like being held, whereas a cat or dog would be fine with it.

What are Rabbits Like in Behavior?

Rabbits hardly conform to their cute and cuddly stereotype in the media. Kits and many young adult rabbits love to constantly dash about and will squeeze themselves into tight spaces. They will chew on exposed boards and food and water dishes. They tend to have rather unique personalities, and you may encounter a few temperamental ones too.

How Do Rabbits Socialize and Warn About Danger?

Rabbits will sniff, groom, and nuzzle other rabbits and may nip each other playfully. Rabbits drum with their hind legs when they sense danger. The drumming of one rabbit can reduce a relaxed herd into individuals frantically running for cover.

I Don't Want My Rabbits Anymore! Can I Set Them Free?

Under no circumstances should domesticated rabbits be set free if rabbit keepers no longer have a use for them. If you no longer want your herd, sell the animals to another breeder, or as pets. Domesticated rabbits have a hard time surviving in the wild. Releasing domesticated animals into the wild is viewed as abandonment, which is an illegal practice.

FEEDING RABBITS

Rabbits are herbivores and are built for a diet consisting mainly of leaves, grass, and some flowers and fruits. Grass hay is a vital part of a rabbit's diet. Grass Hay is an important source of fiber and nutrients to rabbits and keeps their digestive systems functioning normally. Considering that a rabbit can poop up to 300 times a day, the importance of a healthy gut can't be overstated. Grass hay should be available at all times. Most rabbits can comfortably devour a pile of hay the size of themselves each day. Examples of grass hay that rabbits love include: timothy hay, oat, ray, meadow, barley, and Bermuda grasses. These nutritious grasses should be available to rabbits at all times for three main reasons:

- It encourages a healthy digestive system.
- These grasses help to wear down the rabbit's teeth through chewing.
- Keeps rabbits fuller for longer, cutting down on feed costs.

Grass hay can be fed to rabbits from 12 weeks old, but it is recommended to feed a variety to your rabbits. Two or more different types of grass hay will help to provide them with ample nourishment. When selecting grass hay, opt for sun-dried hay over commercially dried hay as it retains more nutrients. Feed a rabbit a pile of hay that is comparable to his own size.

Steer clear from legume hays such as alfalfa and clover. While these hays have more calories, calcium, and protein than regular hay, they can trigger digestive problems and obesity in rabbits. It is not recommended to mix grass hay and legume hay either.

Straw is not a good feed option because it is devoid of nutrients. If straw makes up a key part of a rabbit's diet it can lead to severe nutritional deficiencies.

Green Foods

Green foods such as dandelion greens, collard greens, romaine lettuce, kale, broccoli, parsley, and celery introduce a broader selection of nutrients and water into a rabbit's diet. It is important to include these green foods since rabbits may not drink as much water as they should. These foods can be fed to rabbits older than 12 weeks. It is advised to grow your own greens to feed rabbits as they need at least three varieties of greens daily.

Fruit And Vegetables

Fruit and vegetables should be considered treats. Rabbits can eat too many fruits and vegetables. As counterintuitive as it sounds, large portions of vegetables can have a negative effect on the rabbits' digestive system and can lead to obesity. Try not to feed each rabbit more than a quarter cup of vegetables per day. Think of vegetables as the rabbits' daily vitamin and mineral supplement: healthy in moderation, but troublesome if you overdo it. It is a healthier and cost-effective option than commercial rabbit treats, which tend to be high in starch and fat. Some treats rabbits love include apples, squash, pineapple, carrots, cranberries, cherries, blueberries, blackberries, raspberries, green or red bell peppers, and mango. Rabbits can eat dried fruits, but the amount should be reduced to one-third of the normal amount.

Steer clear from bananas and grapes. Rabbits can become hooked on these foods and may refuse to eat anything else.

Pellets

In ideal conditions, commercial pellets will make up no more than 10% of an adult rabbit's diet. Rabbits under 12 weeks will have a higher percentage of pellets in their diet. Unlike grass hay, pellets do not give rabbits a feeling of fullness, making it easy to overfeed them. Additionally, pellets do not promote healthy and normal tooth wear, which can lead to behavioral and health problems in rabbits. Pellets should be fresh. Check expiration dates and ensure that pellets are not older than two months.

Rabbits are most active at dusk and dawn, so it is best to reserve pellet feeds for this time of day. Feed each rabbit half a cup of pellets and ensure plenty of fresh water is available for the animals. Feed costs can easily be supplemented by selling a few rabbits when needed. In the winter, it is advisable to feed rabbits two-thirds of a cup of pellet feed as they will burn more calories in the cold.

Choosing the Right Feed

Choosing a reliable feed from a sea of options can be overwhelming. Many brands promise that their feed contains "natural ingredients" or that the feed is "fortified with vitamins." Marketing tactics will do your rabbits no favors, so it is best not to be drawn in by it. Examine the label instead!

- *Fiber:* Pelleted feed containing a minimum of 18% fiber will help to keep their digestion healthy.
- *Protein:* Levels of 12-14% are suitable for healthy adult rabbits. Rabbits under five months old will need a protein content of at least 16% in their feed to support rapid growth.
- *Calcium and Phosphorus Ratio:* A calcium content ranging from 0.5–1% is acceptable, while phosphorus should be in the vicinity of 0.4– 0.8%. Look for a ratio of 1.5:2.1 calcium to phosphorus.
- *Fat:* The fat content in feed should be minimal, ranging between 2.4–5%.
- *Vitamins:* Vitamins A, D, and E are of main concern here. A quality feed will contain 1000 IU/kg of Vitamin D, 10,000 IU/kg of Vitamin A, and 50 IU/kg of Vitamin E.
- *Ingredients:* The ingredients list will reveal another important clue: the proportion of ingredients used. Ingredients that are used the most will appear first in the list. It is advised to look for brands that list grass hays or "forage" ahead of cereals like wheat, corn, and oats.

Foods that are grass-based tend to be more nutritionally balanced and are better received by rabbits.

Foods to Never Feed Rabbits

Starchy and fatty foods should never be fed to rabbits. These foods include beans, cereals, bread, chocolate, corn, nuts, oats, refined sugar, seeds, all grains, and peas. Unless instructed by a veterinarian, it is not necessary to feed rabbits any nutritional supplements as misuse of supplements can lead to severe health issues.

Wood to Encourage Tooth Wear

Rabbits gnaw on hard objects to wear down their constantly growing teeth. To help the rabbits in their plight (and discourage unwanted destruction of wooden panels), freshly cut branches can be presented. Keep in mind that not all wood is safe. Never give rabbits apricot, cherry, avocado, plum, peach, cedar, or pine branches as they are potentially harmful.

Rabbits can be safely presented with apple, ash, hazel, pear, poplar, willow, birch, and maple branches. Berry brambles are safe as well.

RABBIT CARE FAQ

Many people mistakenly believe that rabbits are low-maintenance animals with short lifespans. The truth is rabbits require a specialized diet consisting of grass hay, greens, pellets, and treats. With proper care, rabbits can live up to a decade and some large breeds have been known to live longer, but breeders will need to keep a watchful eye on their animals and understand their behaviors. Changes in the rabbits' eating and pooping behavior can signal health issues that will need veterinary intervention. Many health and behavioral issues are preventable with proper care and this will answer some questions about rabbit care.

What Do I Feed Kits?

Kits have very sensitive digestive systems and their needs will change as they grow. For the first three weeks, a kit is dependent on its mother's milk. At the three-week mark, when kits start to explore, pellet feed can be safely introduced. It is advisable to feed kits exclusively pellets until they are 12 weeks old. Everything a growing kit needs is in the feed and they can suffer from diarrhea if they don't remain on a strict diet during this period. The doe's milk and the pellets will provide all the vitamins and minerals kits need to develop a healthy body.

Can I Foster a Rabbit With Cow Milk?

Absolutely not. Cow milk makes for a poor replacement that can result in kit death. If kits need to be fostered, the best rabbit milk alternative is kitten formula, goat's milk, or puppy formula. Fostered kits will need to be fed twice a day and their feed should be adjusted to their stage of growth. The guideline below indicates how much milk a single kit needs, head to *Kit Care Guideline* for more details.

- Newborns need 2.5 ml.
- Week-old kits need 6-7 ml.
- Feed two-week-old kits 12-13 ml.
- Kits from three to six weeks old will need 15 ml.

What Should I Feed Nursing Does?

Pelleted feed containing 18% protein will help nursing does produce milk. In addition to pellets, a lactating doe should have free access to food and water. Supplement her diet with veggies as well.

Can I Make My Own Feed?

Absolutely! Many experienced breeders make their own feed mix or cut out the pellet feed completely if applicable. Another nutritious supplement for rabbits is fodders. Fodders are sprouted grains that are filled with nutrition, making them ideal winter supplements when fresh vegetables and greens are hard to come by. Fodders can be provided daily if the breeder's intention is to replace pellet feed altogether. Keep in mind that fodders should be at least seven inches in height before presenting to rabbits as feed.

Growing fodders is easy. You'll only need three basic items: barley grains, a sprouting tray, and water. Barley grains are quick-growing and transform into lush grass within 10 days. If greens are fed free choice, breeders can safely reduce the amount of pelleted feed by half with no adverse effects on rabbit performance (Cheeke et al., 2000).

Can I Feed Rabbits Without Pellets?

Rabbits will do well without pellets provided the breeder can supply a balanced ration of foods that meets the animal's nutritional requirements. When going pellet-free, the basis of the rabbit's diet should be non-GMO grass hay along with high-protein forages. The grass hay should be a free choice and can be supplemented with rabbit-safe greens, grass clippings, fodder trays, herbs, berries, brambles, and vegetables. The available foods will change with the seasons. When going this route, provide each enclosure with a miner-alized salt ring. Whatever the doe eats, the kits can safely eat too. Without nutrient-rich pellets, the risk of dysbiosis in kits is reduced when strictly grass-feeding rabbits. Rabbits that are fed in this manner might grow a touch slower but will develop lean and healthy bodies.

Why Is My Rabbit Eating Poop?

Rabbits are coprophagous or pseudo-ruminants. This means they eat their own poop so that they can get more of the nutrients from it. From a human perspective, it sounds gross, but there's a method behind the madness. Rabbits have a diet that is fibrous and rich in cellulose, which is not easy to digest. The grass that passes through a rabbit's intestines still contains much of the nutrients it needs, to solve this problem, nature equipped rabbits with a special kind of digestion: hindgut fermentation (McVean, 2018). This allows rabbits to make the most of their meal when ingesting cecotropes (the droppings that rabbits eat). Think of it as the rabbit equivalent to cows chewing their cud. If you spot something that looks like a small, shiny bunch of grapes in the rabbit's enclosure, there's no cause for worry. That's a cecotrope. The presence of multiple cecotropes can signal illness or an inappropriate diet. In these cases, it is best to consult your vet for advice.

Can Rabbits Be Left Alone for a Couple of Days?

Rabbits depend on their keeper for their daily food and water needs. If you stay away from the rabbitry for longer than 24 hours the rabbits may grow anxious, stressed, and can become sick.

Is Regular Tap Water Safe for Rabbits?

Tap water is generally safe for human consumption, so it can be given to rabbits without complications. Keep in mind that rabbits may not drink readily if the water is smelling strongly of chemicals.

Do Rabbits Get Bored With Their Food?

If a rabbit is hutch-bound and does not play or exercise, it can grow bored with its food. As a result, the rabbit may stop eating which can lead to serious health complications. When designing a hutch or any rabbit enclosure, always ensure that rabbits have enough space to move and play.

Why Is My Rabbit Dropping Food?

Rabbits that salivate excessively and drop food while they eat may need to have their teeth trimmed. This problem is preventable in many cases with proper care. Contact your vet for advice in these cases.

How Do I keep Rabbits cool in the heat?

Rabbits are not built to handle the heat well. They cannot sweat and are covered in heavy fur. They may begin to feel uncomfortable when temperatures reach upwards of 65 degrees even, so keeping them cool is vital. If temperatures rise past 90 degrees a rabbit is at risk of heat stroke. A breeder's first line of defense against the heat is a simple one: keep the rabbitry in a shady, well-ventilated area. It is advisable to have rabbitries face east. That way, rabbits will receive their daily dose of the morning sun but remain shielded from the harsh midday heat. Fans can be used to keep rabbits cool. A simple solar panel and small fan system can be set up fairly easily. If the mercury keeps rising, place frozen water bottles in the rabbit enclosure for them to lie next to. Some breeders place ice in the rabbits' drinking water as well. Some breeders use marble tiles as resting boards.

How Do I keep Rabbits warm in the Winter?

Rabbits can withstand cold temperatures way better than hot, however, in extreme weather conditions, it may be necessary to relocate the hutch or enclosure to a shed. Breeders should check the roofs of their enclosures to ensure it is in good condition and waterproof. Any wooden panels inside the hutch should be dry and free from mold. Some breeders use chew-proof heat pads to provide rabbits with extra warmth when the temperature drops below zero. Insulate sleeping and hiding areas with cardboard if need be and give your rabbits plenty of straw to snuggle up in. To keep an icy wind or snowfall out, cover up the run or hutch with a tarp or heavy plastic, but make sure to leave air pockets so rabbits won't suffocate!

Now that you have a better understanding of how to feed and handle rabbits, the next tentative step towards a sustainable rabbitry can be taken—breeding. More on this in the next chapter.

4

BREEDING AND REPRODUCTION

R abbits can be bred year-round, giving credence to the expression "breed like a rabbit." These animals are notorious for being fertile from a young age. Not a lot of human intervention, if any, is required, but it is prudent to wait until the animals reach full maturity before breeding. The age at which rabbits are ready to reproduce depends on the size of the breed. Smaller breeds tend to mature faster than larger breeds, but generally, we can start breeding rabbits at these ages:

Breeding Age	Breed Size	Rabbit Weight At Maturity
4½ months	Small	Under six pounds.
6 months	Medium to large.	6–11lbs., depending on breed.
9 months	Giant	11lbs. or more.

Bucks tend to lag a month behind does in maturing. This means breeders will need to wait if they want to mate a certain buck and doe. While the doe may be ready at 4½ months, it is best to wait an extra month for her buck to fully mature. Waiting is worth it as complications can arise from animals that are bred too early. When selecting breeding pairs, choose animals that are similar in size. Breeding a small doe with a large buck can result in a difficult pregnancy and the kits may be too large for the doe to carry. It is best to breed individuals of the same breed, as cross-breeding requires in-depth knowledge to perform without harming the doe.

Never breed kits from the same litter with each other. Inbreeding of this nature can result in sickly and poor-performing livestock. Some avid practitioners of cuni-culture practice in-line breeding to amplify desirable traits of the breeding pair. In-line breeding happens when a rabbit is bred back to the doe or buck that produced it. There is one caveat: if in-line breeding is not done carefully, undesirable traits can be amplified or introduced into the offspring. This practice is not recommended for novices, as it requires considerable knowledge and experience to implement successfully. Fortunately, rabbit breeding is not all that complicated and novices can achieve impressive results when they understand how rabbit romance works.

Some preparations will need to be made if you want to set the mood for your breeding pair. Breeding is best done on solid ground. Rabbit's feet and toenails can catch in wire-bottomed cages, resulting in injury if the pair is rambunctious. Placing a temporary wooden floor at the bottom of the buck's cage will solve this problem. Also, it is best to remove feeders and water bottles. Frisky rabbits can get tangled up in these. Always remember: the doe goes to the buck's cage, not the other way around. Does are territorial and may act aggressively against bucks in their enclosure.

MATING RABBITS

Once the doe has been placed in the buck's cage, it's normal to observe some chasing, smelling, or stomping of feet. There may be some biting from the buck after he mounts the doe. It's his way of keeping her in place. If a doe is receptive to the buck's advances, she'll lift for him. If she's not ready she'll sit and hide her bottom from the buck.

Shortly after placing the doe in the buck's cage, he will make his first of three attempts to mount her. A buck is a dramatic fellow and he'll tell you if the mission was successful by falling off the doe. It's often preceded by a squeal or grunt. In a bit, he will try again. Good bucks will get the job done fast.

It is advised that the breeder stay nearby for at least two of the attempts. This is to make sure that the doe is not being aggressive or hurting the buck. After the buck finished with his three attempts, remove the doe and return her to her enclosure. Reset the buck's cage and ensure he has plenty of fresh water. If a buck never falls off the doe, it is a sign that the breeding attempt was unsuccessful.

The doe may act aggressively towards the buck and vice versa. In these cases, it is best to remove the doe quickly. You wouldn't want to be trapped in a room with someone you don't have chemistry with, and it's the same for rabbits. Don't force the rabbits to stay in the same cage, it can result in injuries and possible fatality.

Can I Breed Wild Rabbits With Domestic Rabbits?

No. Cottontails and domestic rabbits are two different species and have different chromosome counts. It is unlikely that any kits would survive from such a union.

It is not advised to expose your herd to wild rabbits as these animals can transmit diseases to each other that have the potential to decimate wild and domestic herds.

HANDLING UNRECEPTIVE DOES

Sometimes rabbits need a little helping hand to get in the mood. Whether it is a stubborn doe or a rough buck, several things can catch novice rabbit breeders unaware. Always wait for rabbits to mature before breeding. You can check if a female is ready by the color of her vent. Bright pink indicates she's ready to breed, while purple shows that the egg cycle is coming to an end. A pale vent means that the rabbit is not ready to breed yet—check back on them in a few days. Fortunately, there are a few things a breeder can do when a doe refuses to be bred.

- Try giving her 12–14 hours of light. This can be done by clamping a LED lamp outside the cage. The idea is to trigger the pineal gland, tricking the rabbit's brain into thinking it is breeding season.
- Add apple cider vinegar to the doe's drinking water for a week. One to two tablespoons of apple cider vinegar per gallon of drinking water should be used. Feed this water to an

unreceptive doe or buck to help them get into
the breeding mood.

- Try feeding the doe and buck some sunflower
seeds or oats. Feed the rabbits no more than
five seeds per portion for a maximum of five
days. Peel the seeds before giving it to them.
Rabbits can choke on sunflower seed shells. If
you are feeding oats, limit the serving to one
teaspoon per day.

- Perform a cage swap and leave the doe in the
buck's cage overnight. Swapping the doe and
buck's cage for the night can help to smooth
things along after a failed attempt. The doe will
have time to warm up to the buck's scent,
increasing the chances that she'll cooperate and
lift for him.

- Sometimes a change of scenery can help to
encourage breeding.

When breeding, it is natural for the buck to pull, nip
and nudge at the doe. It encourages her participation.
Sometimes, he can be too rough for the doe's liking,
though. When a buck becomes too rough, try
distracting them by throwing a treat into the cage. She
may change her mind and chances are, he will stop
being rough.

PREGNANCY

A veterinarian can tell you for sure if a doe is pregnant or not, but may not prove a practical option. There are signs that breeders rely on to tell if a rabbit is pregnant or not.

- Gently palpate the rabbit's abdomen and you may feel babies. Use a light touch.
- Weigh the rabbit before she's bred and note the weight. Weigh her again in two weeks. If she's gained weight then she's likely pregnant.
- Rabbits will start to nest a week before kindling. At this point, the doe should be provided with a nesting box.

Does will hop about the enclosure gathering hay, grasses, and tufts of fur to build a nest with. Does will reject nesting boxes if it smells like other rabbits or animals. Clean nesting boxes long before they are given to does, and give them enough time to get used to the box in her enclosure. The doe will start to make her nest when her time draws near.

GESTATION AND KINDLING

Gestation in rabbits ranges from 28 to 31 days. If there are no kits born by day 35 then repeat the breeding process. If you find that you consistently are not having successful breeding and pregnancies then it may be that either the buck or the doe is overweight. Refrain from handling the doe often during this time and leave her nesting box undisturbed.

The doe will need a touch more feed during this time, but don't overfeed her. Overfeeding can lead to miscarriages. Gradually increase the doe's food ration and provide plenty of grass hay and water to keep her in good condition.

A week before kindling the doe will pull fur from her coat and add it to the nest. Some does start pulling fur as early as two weeks, while others do hasty work shortly before kindling. Pulling fur can be a false alarm, though. False pregnancies in rabbits are nothing to be alarmed about. The doe could be mimicking the behavior of pregnant does nearby, or the behavior could be due to a miscarriage.

Caring for the Doe During and After Pregnancy

Does tend to go into labor in the evenings, or when nobody is around to disturb them. Give your doe some privacy when she starts pulling fur. A stressed doe can miscarry or eat her young. Continue keeping your distance, but ensure that the doe has plenty of fresh water after kindling. The doe will clean herself and care for the kits instinctively. She won't be in the nesting box at all times but will nurse the kits when needed.

The doe will do all the heavy lifting, so let nature take its course. She will feed and warm the kits as needed and wean them when the time is right. The only thing the rabbit handler needs to worry about is the routine care of the animal.

Kits are born without fur, but the color of their skin will let you know what the color of their fur will be. Usually, kits open their eyes when they are 10 days old and will hop out of the nest at two weeks of age.

Possible Complications

Kindling can go wrong. There are several common complications rabbit keepers should be aware of. Knowing how to handle these complications can help to increase the productivity of the rabbitry.

Doe Eating Babies

Long-term rabbit breeders have witnessed this ghastly sight at least once. Cannibalism in animals can happen for many reasons, but most of the time, a lack of motherhood characteristics in the doe can be pointed to as the root cause. Don't worry! The doe won't get sick if she's cannibalized her young. If live kits remain, try to foster them with a different nursing doe. Fostering is tricky though, so choose your adoptive rabbit carefully. Some breeds take to fostering kinder than others, so researching your chosen rabbit breed beforehand is vitally important. Unsuccessful fostering attempts can lead the doe to kill all the kits in the nest, hers included (Pieper, 2019).

Kindling Outside the Box

Don't be alarmed if you find kits strewn around the cage of first-time mothers. Perhaps, they did not know where to kindle or what to do with the kits. Some does build beautiful nests, only to kindle on the cage floor. These things happen from time to time. If any babies are alive, pick them up and place them back in the nesting box. If the babies are cold, warm them in your hands or under a heat lamp before returning to the nest.

Too Many Kits

Sometimes does can have litters that are too big for them to handle. In these cases, the runts of the litter will wind up starving to death. To prevent this scenario, some breeders make use of foster does.

Miscarriage and Infections

Complications can arise any time before, during, and after birth. Rabbit keepers are encouraged to watch for lethargy and diminished food and water intake and monitor signs of potential illness on veterinary advice. Sick rabbits should be quarantined away from healthy ones.

Miscarriages can happen for many reasons but the main contributors are poor nutrition, stress, weather conditions, and illness. Dead fetuses should be removed from the doe's cage for hygiene reasons.

5

KIT CARE GUIDE

Tip! Don't name the kits. Naming them makes it a lot harder to harvest them when they come of age. Breeders should check on the kits every day, counting each. It is not uncommon for a kit to die for one reason or the other, so rabbit keepers are advised to check on the litter every day for the first week. Any dead kits should be removed. Be on the lookout for weak kits. Those kits will barely respond to being handled and have sunken bellies and wrinkly skin. These kits are not being nursed properly. A vet will be able to help in these situations.

When litters are eight and above, does may have a hard time supporting them all. She may abandon the litter. In these cases, the litter will need to be fostered, under the guidance of a vet. Rabbit handlers should keep in mind that fostering kits will not produce the same results. No formula can replicate rabbit milk fully.

The First Eight Weeks

The nesting box is the kits' nursery and toilet until they are strong enough to leave the nest on their own. This means you'll need to clean the box daily and provide clean bedding. At two weeks of age, some kits may start nibbling at pellets, but they are still dependent on the doe's milk for 5-8 eight weeks depending on the breed. During this time the kits will slowly increase their pellet intake and decrease milk consumption. Don't be hasty, though. They are not ready to wean yet and still need the doe's antibody-containing milk to remain healthy. Kits that are weaned too soon can result in a poor harvest.

Additionally, do not feed kits greens at this stage. Kits need to stick to a strict diet of pellets for the first twelve weeks. This helps to avoid digestive complications. When rabbits are three months old, you can safely introduce leafy greens into their diet. Remember, their digestive system is still quite sensitive, so it is best to take it slow. Introduce greens one at a time and in small amounts. Slowly increase the number of greens each day until the desired serving size is reached. This will ensure that nothing is causing an imbalance in the rabbit's digestive system and it gives them time to adjust to the new food. It is best to avoid giving young rabbits any treats at this stage, as their digestive systems are still sensitive. If the food item causes problems, it should be removed as soon as possible. Carrots and kale are good items to start with.

Try to handle the kits as little as possible for the first eight weeks. Until the kits are weaned, they are vulnerable to illness and bacteria. Always wash your hands before handling kits that are under eight weeks old. After kits pass the eight-week mark, rabbit keepers are encouraged to handle the kits frequently as this will lead to tamer adult rabbits (Elliott, 2019).

FOSTERING KITS

In rare cases, human intervention is needed with kit care. Whether it is a single kit or an entire litter that needs fostering, your vet can help out. Fostering can be tricky, but with a little patience and knowledge, it can be done.

- *Kits Need to Stay Warm.* Try to make them a soft, warm nest in a box with clean towels. The idea is to give the kit a place to snuggle into. If you have nesting-wool on hand, feel free to use that as well. Cover the box with a light towel, but leave an inch gap at the top for air. Keep the kits in a quiet area and pay attention to the room temperature.

- *A Room Temperature of 68 to 72 Degrees is Optimal.* If the temperature drops below this, use a heating pad to warm the kits. Set the heating pad on its lowest heat setting and slip half of it under the box. That way the kit can move to the cooler side of the box if need be. Never put kits directly on a heating pad, they'll burn badly.

Feeding Orphaned Kits

Kits should be raised on kitten milk replacers or goat milk. Most kits will refuse to nurse from baby animal bottles. They'll need to be fed with a sterile oral syringe. Feedings should be limited to two times a day, but sometimes more feedings are needed to get an adequate amount into the kits, especially at first.

How much milk to feed the kits varies by breed and age of the kit. The basic guideline below is intended for rabbits that will weigh five pounds on maturity. You may need to adjust the amounts for your rabbit. The amounts below are daily amounts, divide them by two for the feeding amount.

Age of Rabbit	Amount of Formula Daily
Under one week.	4-5 ml
Between one and two weeks old.	10-15 ml
Two to three weeks old.	15-30 ml
Three to six weeks old.	30 ml

Kits feed by while lying on their backs. Loosely wrap a kit in a soft towel. Keep the kit on your lap or in the crook of your arm when feeding. Some kits may refuse to eat, and that's fine. Simply do the best you can, but let the kit eat at its own pace. Syringe-feeding requires a light touch, you don't want to squirt the liquid too quickly down their throats, as they will suffocate.

The first ten days are a crucial period. You'll need to keep an eye on the kits to see if they develop any stomach problems. If you notice the kit is not relieving itself normally, you can help it out by copying what the doe would do. In situations like these, the doe will lick the kit to encourage it to relieve itself. A soft cloth or moistened cotton ball (make sure it is warm) can be used to gently stroke the rabbit in the genital area. This should be done until the kit goes to the bathroom and can be stopped when the kit does. The stool may be in varying shades of green and yellow. Keep an eye on the urine. If it is brown and gritty the rabbit is dehydrated and may need a vet immediately. Be sure to keep the kit's mouth clean and that no milk dries in their hair.

Kits usually open their eyes at the 10-day mark. At this point introduce them to pellets. Leave some in the corner of their box along with some water. Use a shallow water dish and fill it frequently to prevent drowning. Continue to adjust the kit's feed as it grows. Kits can be weaned from as early as six weeks, but it is recommended to wait until eight weeks before weaning.

SEXING RABBITS

Sexing rabbits is a tricky task. It is best to start when the kits are four weeks old, as they would be more developed, saving rabbit handlers some frustration. Here's how it's done:

- Place your hand under the rabbit's stomach. Be gentle, yet firm.
- Roll the rabbit back on its butt, supporting the body as you do this.
- Gently press on the pelvic area until the cone protrudes. If the rabbit is a buck, the tube will

be round and pink with a hole at the end. Does have an oval shape with a slit. It takes some practice to spot the difference, especially in young rabbits! If you are unsure of a kit's gender, check again in a few days.

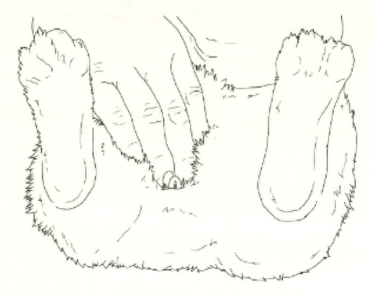

Female- Doe

Male-Buck

A good doe will give you minimal worries over kits; however, breeders need to be aware of basic rabbit first aid and disease prevention to get the most out of their herd. I'll cover these topics in the next chapter.

6

FIRST AID AND DISEASE PREVENTION

This information is here for educational purposes and is not intended to diagnose, treat or prevent disease. Please make contact with an animal health professional. Having healthy, hardy rabbits starts in the beginning. Only buy healthy animals with good breeding lines. And continue to breed in hardy traits. If you don't, their litter will inherit those traits. Cull out rabbits that show weakness or illness. In doing this, you will have very few problems with diseases.

Quarantining Rabbits

Unless you are living in South Africa, there's good reason to quarantine any new rabbit you acquire for 30 days. South Africa is among a handful of countries that are free of two major diseases in rabbits, namely Myxomatosis and Viral Hemorrhagic Disease (Steenekamp, n.d.). Waiting one month before breeding that prized buck or newly acquired doe will save rabbit keepers a lot of headaches.

Quarantining does not mean housing the rabbit on the other end of the enclosure. That defeats the purpose. Ideally, a separate room or enclosure will be used for quarantine purposes. Keep in mind that quarantine rabbits will be fed and watered last. Refrain from handling your other rabbits until you have washed up. The idea is to prevent the transmission of viruses and bacteria. If the rabbit shows signs of illness during the quarantine period, get it treated. When all the symptoms have cleared, quarantine the rabbit for an additional 30 days.

Care for the quarantined rabbit as per routine and maintain a clean environment. Clean cage floors well between litters. The cage floor can be torched or cleaned with a spray solution of 90% water and 10% bleach.

SPOTTING SICK RABBITS

A healthy rabbit has bright eyes, dry nostrils, and a clean, shiny coat. These rabbits are alert and their droppings tend to be small pellets. For rabbits that show any signs of illness or suddenly behave strangely, it is best to call a vet. Trouble is, that vets specializing in rabbit care and rabbit-specific medicine can be hard to find. Oftentimes, it is hard to spot a sick rabbit early on, as they may not show any signs of illness until they are very ill. Sick rabbits can worsen very quickly, so it is best to act as soon as you spot a rabbit that is under the weather. Signs of illness in rabbits include:

- Behavior changes, such as hunching up or sitting still. Eating and drinking habits may be affected as well and the rabbit may have a lack of appetite or drink more water than normal. Rabbits may exhibit aggression or display behaviors that indicate they want to be left alone more regularly.
- A swollen limb or an abnormal gait points to possible injury and can be the result of fighting or insect bites.
- The rabbit is leaking from its eye, ears, or nose or experiences stomach problems, such as difficulty in relieving itself or diarrhea.
- Droppings that are soft pellets are a sign that all is not well with the rabbit.
- The rabbit may experience signs of pain and may not take kindly to certain parts of its body

being touched. In addition, the rabbit may grind its teeth, flinch or have difficulty breathing (especially if it's breathing through its mouth).

- If the breeder spots redness on the skin around the rabbit's belly, bottom, or underside of the feet, it is a sure sign that the animal is unwell.

Should a Rabbit Be Culled?

Culling is removing the animal from the herd. Culling is important to keep the herd healthy, but we need to differentiate between soft and hard culling here. With soft culling, the rabbit is removed from the herd but remains alive. It is typically quarantined or may require special care that justifies its removal from the herd. Hard culling is the act of euthanizing the rabbit and is usually done to end the suffering of an animal that can't be helped.

ROUTINE HEALTH CHECK

A routine health check can save rabbit handlers the pain of starting their herd anew. Giving your herd a routine health check will help you spot signs of illness relatively early on and can prevent the entire herd from being wiped out. A responsible rabbit keeper will perform a series of daily and weekly checks and quarantine sickly individuals immediately to keep their herd in top condition.

Eight Daily Checks

Daily checks can easily be performed when a rabbit keeper goes about the daily care and maintenance of the enclosure or hutch. Keep an observant eye on:

- **Behavior:** The rabbit should be eating and drinking normally.
- **Feet:** Bald patches and sores are a clear indicator that the rabbit will need resting boards.
- **Coat:** Parasites, bald patches, dandruff, sores, scaly patches, damp or weeping patches and wounds are cause for concern and should be treated as soon as possible.
- **Mouth:** Signs of dribbling can indicate overgrown teeth and will need veterinary intervention.
- **Eyes:** Runny and weeping eyes are often signs that the rabbit is suffering from dental problems or respiratory infections.
- **Nose:** A runny nose is a sign of respiratory infection that can easily turn into pneumonia if left untreated.
- **Ears:** Check for any crusty wax inside the ear.

- *Bottom:* Check the rabbit's bottom and the floor of its living area. If signs of diarrhea or urine staining are present the rabbit will need to see a vet quickly (Ni Direct Government Services, 2015).

Four Weekly Checks

In addition to daily checks, rabbit keepers need to keep an eye on the animal's nails, teeth, mouth, and weight to ensure it remains in optimal health. These checks can be performed alongside the routine care of the animals.

- *Nails:* Check that the nails are not damaged and that it is a suitable length.
- *Teeth:* The front teeth should be in good shape and of a suitable length. A rabbit's back teeth should be checked once a year, but this can only be done by a veterinarian.
- *Mouth:* A wet chin or drooling is a sign that something is not right with the animal, but it can be difficult to spot as rabbits keep themselves clean. Check for stains on the fur of their chest and the inside of their front paws.
- *Weight:* Weigh rabbits once a week. Rabbits that have lost weight may suffer from dental or health problems. Rabbits that have gained weight might be pregnant or overweight. Since

rabbits have a fine bone structure, being overweight can cause serious health problems for the animal.

Keep in mind that during warm weather, you'll need to check under the rabbit and around its bottom for droppings twice a day. A dirty bottom increases the risk of fly strike, which can kill rabbits in hours. Flies will lay their eggs in the rabbit's soiled fur, the maggots will hatch, and proceed to eat into the rabbit's flesh. Not only is it incredibly painful, but it releases toxins into the rabbit's bloodstream. This produces a state of shock, and severe illness and can result in death, therefore any wounds or injuries on rabbits will need to be checked daily. If you spot any maggots on the animal, contact your vet immediately.

RABBIT FIRST AID GUIDE

Being able to handle emergencies in a calm manner is a crucial skill rabbit handlers need to learn. It only takes a few moments to assess an animal for signs of bleeding or injury. Keeping a basic first aid kit on hand can make the difference between saving rabbits and culling them. The first aid kit should contain:

- Bandage material is to be used if a rabbit is bleeding and needs to be transported to the vet.
- Antimicrobial cream for superficial wounds.
- Antimicrobial wash.
- Nail clippers, but only if you are confident in using them. It is very easy to cut rabbit nails too close, cutting into the flesh, also called the quick, resulting in pain, bleeding, and discomfort for the animal. Don't be surprised if the rabbit makes noises or tries to bite in these cases. Calm the animal and staunch the bleeding the best you can. Depending on the severity of the bleeding, it may be necessary to seek the help of a vet.

In the event of an emergency, try to call ahead to the vet's office if it does not delay treatment. This will help to give the veterinary team a head start so they can provide the best possible chance of recovery for the animal. Certain situations require rabbit keepers to approach them differently to ensure the best chances of recovery.

- *The Rabbit Is Bleeding:* Depending on the amount of blood, a rabbit handler may need to intervene to stem the bleeding before taking the animal to a vet for assessment. If the blood is trickling or pumping, it is best to cover the area with clean bandage material and apply pressure. Don't use tissue, it can get stuck in the wound and cause more trouble.

- *Rabbit Is Wounded:* Wounds may need covering and may justify moving the rabbit into a clean box for transportation to the vet. If you spot something sticking out of the wound, do not remove it. You'd risk worsening the bleeding and increasing injury to the rabbit. Small puncture wounds can pose a problem too as they can form abscesses that can lead to severe illness.

- *Limping Or Broken Bones:* A limping rabbit or one with broken bones should be placed into a secure carrier box for transport to the vet. Don't chase the rabbit when trying to get it into the carrier, it will make the injury worse. Place a towel over the rabbit and gently lift it into the box, and make sure to support any broken limbs in the process.

- *Broken Nails:* Unless you are confident in trimming rabbit nails, don't cut these yourself. It is easy to injure rabbits by cutting into the quick.

- *The Rabbit Collapsed:* In these cases, check the airway, breathing, and circulation of the animal.

Check the mouth for any debris, be careful as the rabbit could bite. Watch for signs of breathing and place one hand under the chest to feel for a heartbeat. If the rabbit doesn't have a heartbeat or is not breathing, phone the vet immediately. There are many reasons why a rabbit would collapse: heat stroke, heart issues, breathing difficulties, stress, pain, or gut issues. Don't feel too troubled if you can't identify right away why the rabbit collapsed, the most important thing here is to get veterinary advice as soon as possible.

FIRST LINE TREATMENT FOR COMMON PROBLEMS

Some common problems in rabbits can be prevented when handlers have a healthy understanding of a rabbit's needs. Always quarantine a sick or injured animal from the rest of the herd to prevent unnecessary losses.

- *Small Wounds:* Small wounds and wounds from fighting can be treated topically with hydrogen peroxide, Neosporin, or Vetericyn.
- *Snuffles (Pasteurellosis):* The *Pasteurella multocida* bacteria can easily be transferred

from one rabbit to another via contact. The bacteria commonly affect the eyes and nose but can cause head tilt when infecting the ears. This bacterium also causes abscesses and uterine infections. Preventing the snuffles is as simple as keeping your rabbits calm and relaxed. Some strains of *Pasteurella* can remain latent in the rabbit's nose, only to flare up when the animal is stressed. This often occurs when a new rabbit is introduced, overcrowding in the enclosure, or when rabbits are on a new diet. Quarantine the rabbit and keep it as stress-free as possible to manage the signs and keep the rest of the herd healthy. If need be, your vet will prescribe antibiotics or recommend surgery if an abscess forms.

- *Preventing Hairballs:* Rabbits love to keep themselves clean, in this aspect they are a lot like cats. Just like cats, they tend to suffer from hairballs if a keeper neglects routine grooming. The frequency of grooming will depend on the length of their coats. Short-haired rabbits can be brushed once or twice a week, while longer-haired animals may need daily brushing to prevent hairballs. Some breeds are more prone to hairballs than others, but a daily helping of grass hay along with regular grooming and exercise will keep this problem at bay. Long-haired breeds like Angora rabbits, Lionheads, and Jersey Woolies are at an elevated risk of suffering from hairballs due to the length of their coats and will need extra grooming and care. Rabbits can't spit up hairballs as cats do and breeders will need to keep an eye out for signs of improper digestion to determine if a rabbit is suffering from a hairball.

- **Nest Box Eyes:** Place a warm wet washcloth on their eye for just a bit to loosen the crust. Gently work the eye open, and wipe around the eye to work out pus. Watch the eyes closely for a couple of days, repeating the washing process twice a day. If it doesn't resolve in two days, use Terramycin topically.

- **Sore Hocks:** Most common in overweight rabbits. It is so important that your rabbits stay trim and healthy. It is a myth that wire flooring causes sore hocks. The best gauge for flooring tends to be galvanized 1/2 x 1 wire. Always give your rabbit a resting board such as a piece of plywood or marble. To treat sore hocks, clean the area and treat it with lidocaine. Finish off by wrapping the injured foot. Alternatively, Pad Kote can be used.

- *Parasites, Mites, Fleas Ticks, and Ringworm:* Use Ivermectin, either topically or through injections. Never inject rabbits unless your vet prescribes it. Rabbits are sensitive and the wrong injection (or injectable amounts) can kill them. Use a 22–24-gauge needle, 23 gauge can typically be bought at a farm supply store. Your vet will advise how to use Ivermectin correctly. Additionally, a dust bath can be handy to cure mites and fleas.

- *Bacterial Infections:* These are treated with penicillin and an average of 0.1 cc antibiotic is used per pound of rabbit. Many rabbitries use broad-spectrum antibiotics, like Terramycin or duramycin. Don't overuse or use without the guidance of a vet, as it can lead to liver damage. Try to use probiotics to maintain healthy gut bacteria while administering antibiotics. Apple cider vinegar with the mother in it is filled with beneficial bacteria and can be added to their drinking water. Electrolytes and vitamins can be given as well if needed.

Which Antibiotics are Dangerous to Rabbits?

Very few products are recommended for use in rabbits. Particular care needs to be taken around antibiotics, as they can suppress healthy gut microflora which can lead to complications known as antibiotic toxicity. Antibiotics that are not recommended for use in rabbits include clindamycin, lincomycin, erythromycin, ampicillin, amoxicillin/clavulanic acid, and cephalosporins (MSD Veterinary Manual, n.d.).

Clean the cages between litters with a solution of 90% water and 10% bleach. Cage floors can be torched to kill bacteria as well. Scoop out rabbit's excrement regularly if you are following the colony method and put down fresh bedding. Don't use cedar shavings, they might smell nice, but are not healthy for rabbits at all.

HERD DESTROYERS: FATAL RABBIT DISEASES

There are two diseases that rabbit handlers should be wary of, namely: Myxomatosis and Rabbit Hemorrhagic Disease Virus. Mosquitoes play a big role in the spread of these diseases. The best way to protect the herd is by vaccination and investing in mosquito-proof enclosures. We'll take a brief look at what each disease entails.

- *Myxomatosis:* This virus is transmitted by mosquitoes, fleas, or contact with an infected animal. Swelling and discharge from the eyes, nose, and the anogenital tract. Vaccination every 12 months can prevent the disease from setting in, but vaccines may be hard to come by. Your best bet is to mosquito-proof the rabbit enclosure. It is especially important to ensure the animals are sheltered at dawn and dusk, as this is when mosquitoes are most active. Flea control measures should be used, especially when introducing new rabbits into the herd after their quarantine period. Myxomatosis is fatal.

- *Rabbit Haemorrhagic Disease Virus (RHDV):* Mosquitoes are the culprits, but contact with infected animals will cause the disease to spread throughout the herd too. There are four strains of RHDV, but in most mature rabbits the disease progresses rapidly. Within 48 to 72 hours, the rabbit will progress from fever and lethargy to death. The virus has a very short incubation period of one to three days, which accounts for the rapid decline observed in sick rabbits. Sadly, symptoms are hard to spot but can include poor appetite, lethargy, restlessness, and fever. RHDV acutely damages the liver and results in blood-clotting abnormalities. The disease is fatal in most cases. Rabbits can be protected via a vaccine that is administered every six months. There is no treatment available for the disease, so insect control

measures and quarantining are your best tools
to prevent your entire herd from dying off.

Rabbits that are contaminated with Myxomatosis and
RDHV should not be processed or consumed. Think of
these dead animals as a biohazard: they should be safely
discarded via deep burial or disposed of as directed by a
State Animal Health Official.

7

BUTCHERING AND PROCESSING

Harvesting rabbits can be difficult at first. Rabbits are commonly dispatched and butchered once they are eight weeks old or have reached the five-pound mark. This depends on the breed and rabbit keeper. Some keepers prefer to harvest their rabbits between eight and nine weeks, when the meat is tender, while others prefer to harvest at 12 weeks old. Rabbits older than 12 weeks tend to have tougher meat and are only suitable for recipes that call for a long slow cook. Processing rabbits at the right age is important, as they require more feed for smaller weight gains as they age, tipping that delicate feed-to-meat ratio most rabbit handlers try to maintain.

Keep in mind that rabbits slaughtered to be sold to commercial establishments need to be processed in such a way that it meets local or state health codes. These codes are established and enforced by agencies. Sometimes, these agencies have regulatory control, sometimes they don't. It all depends on where you live. Usually, this means that if you intend to sell the meat, it will need to be butchered at an inspected facility. Finding a butcher can be a challenge. In general, rabbit carcasses can be sold when state requirements are met. It is advisable to check with your state meat inspection agency or county agent regarding the policies that govern this process. Rabbits slaughtered for private use are not subject to these regulations.

Preparation is key to starting the harvesting process. These are all tools and supplies one would typically need:

- Sharp skinning knife and knife sharpener.
- Heavy shears and cut-resistant gloves.
- A container for the offal. (Offal is the organs and other waste) -10-gallon buckets work well for this purpose.
- Water for cleaning knives and hands.
- Hopper Popper-for dispatching
- A way to suspend the rabbit while working on it. Maybe two strings hanging from a ceiling, creating two loops for the rabbit's hind legs to hang from.

Don't worry if you don't have these exact items on hand, as most items can be substituted for what you have available in your kitchen. Ensure that your knives are sharp. The Hopper Popper is a tool that is designed for the meat rabbit trade and makes dispatching meat rabbits easier and more humane. If you don't have one on hand, no problem. The job can still be done humanely in an old-fashioned way.

DISPATCHING RABBITS HUMANELY

The taste of rabbit meat will instantly tell you if that animal was dispatched humanely or not. Any stress during the butchering process will release a cocktail of endocrine hormones (including adrenaline) that can and will toughen the meat and negatively affect the flavor. If the meat tastes sweet, like chicken, the animal died humanely. Dispatch methods are detailed below.

The Foolproof Broken Neck

Also called cervical dislocation, breaking the rabbit's neck quickly and cleanly is the preferred method for many keepers. It is believed to minimize any pain and suffering for the animal and results in instant death. The process is practically foolproof and beginner-friendly, all you'll need is a broomstick and a firm grip.

- Place the rabbit on the ground and distract it with a treat.
- Position a broomstick or rod across the rabbit's neck and secure one side by stepping on it. The next step needs to happen quickly, so be prepared.
- Simultaneously step on the other side of the broomstick or rod and pull the rabbit's body

upwards at a 90-degree angle by the hind legs. You'll need to pull hard and quickly to break the neck. It is normal to feel a give and a stretch at this point.

- At this point, death throes will be setting in. Understand that death throes are proof of death, even if the rabbit's eyes open. Open eyes do not mean the animal is aware or feeling pain.
- Using a sharp knife, cut off the rabbit's head through the break in the neck. This should be easy, as you are only cutting through muscle and fur now.
- Hang the rabbit by the hind legs to complete the harvesting process.

Fatal Blow

There's a reason why the rabbit punch is an illegal boxing move. A sharp blow to the base of the skull results in instant death when done correctly. Hunters often use this method to quickly and efficiently dispatch rabbits with a well-placed blow. While the method is humane, it is not foolproof. If the rabbit is not struck hard enough, or in the wrong place it can lead to unnecessary pain and suffering. Always confirm your kill before butchering the animal.

Once dispatched, the rabbit should be hung from the hind legs. This can be done by using two nails on which the feet can be hooked. Tying the legs with a length of string works very well too. Once the rabbit is hanging the next step in harvesting can begin.

Skinning

After the rabbit is hung by its feet and its head has been cut off start by cutting little slits around the feet. Use the knife to separate the skin from the carcass, gently working your way down the leg until it meets the body. You may need to tear the skin gently, working around the tail. Do the same on the other leg and continue to skin the rabbit all the way. Catch any draining blood with the offal bucket and be careful not to nick the flesh while skinning. Once the skin is removed, wash the carcass and remove any remaining hair.

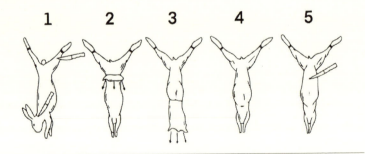

GUTTING

Start at the anus and make a slit down the center of the rabbit. Don't push the knife too deep, or you'll cut into the intestines and sour the meat. Use a slow and shallow cut to maintain maximum control of the knife. As you cut, organs will start to fall out, so aim them towards the offal bucket to keep things tidy. Ensure the cavity of the carcass is empty and cut out the anus. Wash the carcass thoroughly.

The heart, kidneys, and liver can be salvaged and used in a variety of recipes. Always make sure the liver of the animal is healthy. It should be a deep red color. If the liver looks abnormal, is discolored, or has muddled spots, do not eat the meat. Carcasses of animals with unhealthy livers should be disposed of.

BUTCHERING

Place the carcass on a hard, flat surface. We want the carcass lying on its side. Lift a front leg and run the knife along the shoulder blade towards the sternum to separate the leg and shoulder. Keeping the carcass on the same side, remove the hind leg. Begin at the top of the rump and cut down to sever the leg. Joints and bones can be popped out of their sockets if need be. Flip the carcass and repeat the process.

Cut out any pelvic bones that remain once the legs have been removed. The sternum should be split down the middle. Locate and loosen the eye of the loin. You can then separate the rack and saddle and remove any traces of tailbone and belly fat.

When the butchering process is complete, place the meat in a large, clean container full of cold water. Allow it to soak in the fridge for 24 hours to remove any remaining traces of blood.

After soaking, the meat is ready to be stored. Vacuum seal the meat and pop it in the freezer for long-term storage. Alternatively, the meat can be smoked, canned, or dehydrated following your favorite recipe.

MEAT MATH: HOW MANY RABBITS TO FEED A FAMILY

A family of four can eat rabbits five times a week with six breeding does. Of course, these numbers depend on how many fryers per meal are used and can be adjusted to suit your family's needs. The table below compares the number of rabbit dishes with the number of does a breeder could need.

Amount of Rabbit Dishes Per Week	Does Needed If Using One Fryer Per Meal	Does Needed If Using Two Fryers Per Meal
1	2	3
2	3	5
3	4	7
4	5	9
5	6	11
6	7	13
7	8	16

Bear in mind that the table assumes each doe produces 48 fryers annually. Dress-out rates vary and this can influence the amount of meat needed per meal.

8

RABBIT 10 WAYS: DELICIOUS RECIPES TO TRY

R abbit meat has been described as having a taste similar to chicken, only meatier. Rabbit can be substituted into any chicken-based dish with mouthwatering results.

There are many ways to enjoy rabbits. The traditional way of preparing rabbit meat is by braising, stewing, or baking it into a pie or you could try rabbit ragu for a delectable pasta sauce. Your imagination is the only limit here! Always bring chilled meat up to room temperature before cooking. Rabbit is lean, so it needs to rest before serving to retain juiciness. If you are baking it, after seasoning, cover and bake in a 385F oven until the rabbit meat reaches temperatures of 160F or 71C.

Rabbits can be boiled slowly to create shredded meat to be used in tacos, salads, or sliders too Simply place the rabbit in a large pot, and cover it with water or a beer. Bring it to a boil and let it simmer for 90 minutes.

Slow Methods for Succulent Meat

Rabbit has a reputation for being tricky to cook as it dries out easily. Slow cooking is ideal to bring out the flavor and impart tenderness to older rabbits. The meat is slowly tenderized for stews, ragus, terrines, and casseroles. Cooking at low temperatures in liquid is the best option to bring out the best in this meat. Brown the meat before slow cooking to add richness and color to the dish.

Any part of the rabbit can be used in slow cooking. Consider allowing the rabbit to cool in the braising liquid before reheating it later to prevent drying out. Those who love confit will be thrilled to know that rabbits can be confited at low temperatures in oil or duck fat. This ensures the meat stays succulent.

Quick Cooking

Rabbit can be cooked quickly too. Ideally, the meat needs to be jointed first, but once this is done it can be treated like chicken and fried on moderate heat for 20 minutes or until the meat reaches an internal temperature of 160F or 71°C. The saddle and loin are best suited for quick cooking. Other cuts of meat are more suitable for roasting and braising.

How long rabbit meat is roasted depends entirely on the joint. There's little fat on the flesh, so it does not need long cooking times. Many recipes call for a quick sear before roasting it briefly in a hot oven. It is preferable to roast the rabbit on the bone to help it retain moisture and flavor.

Flavors to Compliment Rabbit Meat

Rabbit pairs well with garlic, rosemary, sage, prunes, and salty ham and pancetta. A tangy mustard dressing can enliven the flavor of the meat and it suits cider and cream-based sauces beautifully. If you are feeling experimental or want a taste of rural Italy, try some rabbit in your pasta or serve it with polenta. For lighter meals, a side of spinach, or asparagus, compliments rabbit harmoniously.

Marinating the meat overnight in buttermilk is a great way to sweeten and tenderize the meat. All this talk of food is bound to stir up an appetite, so feel free to dig into these simple, wholesome recipes below:

Casserole-Roasted Whole Rabbit

Italian home cooking at its best, this dish is a perfect introductory recipe for those who never cooked rabbit before. The dish can be made ahead of time.

Serving Size: Makes eight servings.

Cook Time: 140 minutes

Nutritional Information:

Calories	Carbs	Fat	Protein
656	1g	39g	84g

Ingredients:

- Two whole rabbit carcasses weighing 3.5lbs each
- 2 marjoram sprigs
- 4 thyme sprigs (can use 2 tsp of dried herb)
- 2 rosemary sprigs (can use 1 tsp of dried herb)
- 2 sage sprigs (can use 1 tsp of dried herb)
- 2 bay leaves
- 5 tbsp of unsalted butter
- 2 tbsp of extra-virgin olive oil
- 4 thinly sliced garlic cloves
- Half a cup of dry white wine
- A splash of water

- Salt and pepper to taste

Directions:

- Rinse the rabbit and pat dry with paper towels. Stuff equal amounts of thyme, rosemary, sage, bay leaves, and marjoram into the carcass cavity. Seal the cavity with a toothpick.
- Use an enameled casserole dish (cast iron is best) to melt 1.5 tbsp of butter and 1 tbsp of olive oil. Season the rabbits with salt and pepper. Place one rabbit, breast side down, into the casserole and cook on moderately high heat until browned. Turn the rabbit over and brown the other side. It should take eight minutes in total. Transfer the rabbit to a platter, discard the fat and repeat the process with the remaining stuffed rabbit. Reserve a tablespoon of fat.
- Once the rabbit has been browned, use kitchen string to tie the hind legs together. Use the reserved fat to brown the garlic in the casserole. At this point, return the rabbits to the casserole and pour wine in. bring it to a boil, making sure to scrape the sides and bottom of the casserole (that's where all the flavor hides). Add a splash of water and the remaining butter.

- Cover and cook over low heat for 40 minutes. Turn the rabbits once and baste them with the cooking liquid a few times during the cooking process. Preheat the oven to 350°.
- When the oven is heated, place the casserole in the oven and bake for one hour, or until the meat is tender. Turn the rabbits once and baste a few times during cooking.
- After cooking, transfer the meat to a cutting board and remove toothpicks and strings. Cut off the hind legs, tenderloins, and breast flaps and arrange them on a platter. Cover with foil to keep the meat warm.
- Bring the remaining juices in the casserole to a boil over high heat and reduce until half a cup of liquid remains. Transfer the gravy to a bowl and serve.

Roasted Rabbit With Mustard

The spicy notes of this dish pair nicely with a rich, low-tannin red wine. This recipe is the brainchild of former chef, David Tanis, who ran the kitchen of the acclaimed Café Escalera in Santa Fe, New Mexico.

Serving Size: Makes eight servings.

Cook Time: 140 minutes

Nutritional Information:

Calories	Carbs	Fat	Protein
736	2.9g	35.9g	94.3g

Ingredients:

- 5lbs of rabbit
- 4 bay leaves
- 8 cloves of garlic, chopped
- 2 tsp mustard seeds, crushed
- 2 tbsp chopped, fresh thyme
- 3/4 cup mustard, preferably Dijon
- 1.5 cups crème fraîche
- Half a pound of unsmoked bacon or pancetta that is cut into quarter-inch strips
- Salt and pepper to taste

Directions:

- In a deep bowl, season the rabbit with salt and pepper. Pour the remaining ingredients over the meat and mix until all the pieces are coated. Cover the bowl and allow it to marinate for at least one hour at room temperature. The rabbit can be marinated overnight in the fridge.

- Heat the oven to 400°. If the rabbit was in the fridge, allow it to come to room temperature before cooking. Place the meat into a shallow roasting pan and top with the remaining marinade. You may need to use two roasting pans.
- Roast the rabbit for 55 minutes, turning it once and basting it occasionally. At this point, set the oven to broil for 5 minutes to achieve a beautiful golden brown color on the meat.
- Serve and enjoy the meat with the juices from the pan.

Grilled Rabbit

The barbecue and woody herbs transform rabbit meat into a divine delicacy that is super easy to make, especially for novices. If you ever needed an excuse to use the grill, this recipe will help you out!

Serving Size: Makes two servings.

Cook Time: 45 minutes

Nutritional Information:

Calories	Carbs	Fat	Protein
508	4g	37g	39.4g

Ingredients:

- 2.6 lbs. of rabbit, preferably jointed.
- A handful of fresh rosemary and thyme
- 4 cloves of garlic
- 8 tbsp of olive oil
- One lemon, zested and juiced
- A teaspoon of honey
- 4 thick slices of pancetta
- Salt and pepper to taste
- metal or wooden skewers

Directions:

- In a pestle and mortar; pound thyme, rosemary, garlic, and lemon zest to a pulp. Stir in olive oil, lemon juice, and honey. Set aside for a moment. Place the rabbit pieces into a bowl and pour the bashed herbs over. Cover the bowl and allow it to marinate while you light up the barbecue.
- Grab a few sprigs of thyme and tie them into a small bushel. Use this bushel as a basting brush to impart extra flavor to the meat with every turn. Set your makeshift basting brush aside for now.
- Remove the meat from the marinate and receive the liquid. Season the meat with salt and

pepper and a skewer. Sandwich a piece of pancetta between the rabbit meat on the skewer and pop it on the grill, turning and basting regularly until fully cooked.

- Serve with roast potatoes, salads, or white beans.

Kentucky-Inspired Fried Rabbit

Love fried chicken? Then give this fried rabbit a try. Rabbit marinated in buttermilk and fried is tender and moist. The meat will need to marinate overnight for the best result, but it will be worth it. As the cooking method suggests, a young rabbit (fryer) is best suited for this recipe.

Serving Size: Makes four servings.

Cook Time: 10 minutes

Nutritional Information:

Calories	Carbs	Fat	Protein
719	59g	23.2g	64.2g

Ingredients:

- One young, butchered rabbit.
- 2 cups of buttermilk

- 4 cloves of garlic, crushed
- 1 tsp of dried thyme
- 1 tsp of dried oregano
- 1 tsp of dried rosemary
- 1 tsp paprika (regular or smoked works equally well)
- 3 tsp cayenne pepper
- A sliced onion
- 2 cups of flour
- 1 tsp garlic powder
- 1 tsp onion powder
- Salt and pepper to taste
- Oil for frying

Directions:

- Place rabbit in a container (or zip-lock bag) and pour buttermilk, onion, minced garlic, oregano, rosemary, paprika, thyme, and one tsp of cayenne. Mix the ingredients well until fully incorporated, ensuring that the rabbit pieces are coated. Cover the container and marinate in the fridge overnight.
- In a bowl (or zip-lock bag) mix flour, garlic- and onion powder, the remainder of the cayenne pepper, and salt and pepper. Heat three

cups of oil in a large skillet over medium heat to deep-fry the rabbit.

- Remove the rabbit from the marinade. Coat the pieces with the flour mixture. Fry in heated oil for 10 minutes, until golden brown. Place on a wire rack to drain the excess oil and serve.

Rabbit Gumbo

Bold gumbo flavors and savory sausage slices complement the delicate rabbit meat nicely, adding character to a dish that is sure to become a family favorite!

Serving Size: Makes four to six servings.

Cook Time: 140 minutes

Nutritional Information:

Calories	Carbs	Fat	Protein
667	10.5g	43g	56g

Ingredients:

- 3 lbs. of rabbit
- One onion and green pepper, chopped
- 1/4 cup oil
- Half a pound of smoked sausage, cut into quarter-inch pieces

- Salt to taste
- Half a teaspoon dried thyme
- Quarter of a teaspoon pepper
- Quarter of a teaspoon cayenne pepper
- Half a cup sliced okra

Directions:

- Heat oil in a Dutch Oven and sauté onion and green pepper until soft. Add rabbit and brown it slightly. Pour water to cover the meat and allow it to simmer covered for up to two hours (or until the meat is tender).
- Add sausage, salt, pepper, cayenne, and thyme and simmer the mixture uncovered for an additional 20 minutes. Remove the rabbit and debone. Cut the meat into pieces and return it to the Dutch Oven. Stir in okra and bring to a boil for a few minutes.
- Serve over hot rice in deep bowls.

Rabbit Cacciatore

Craving Italian-American flavors but not confident in the kitchen? Don't worry, I've got you covered! In three simple steps, your family could be feasting on delicious Cacciatore.

Serving Size: Makes four to six servings.

Cook Time: 120 minutes

Nutritional Information:

Calories	Carbs	Fat	Protein
892	19g	39g	111g

Ingredients:

- 7 lbs. of rabbit
- 15 oz sliced mushrooms
- One sliced onion
- 15 oz tomato sauce
- Quarter cup of flour
- Garlic salt to taste
- Black pepper to taste
- 2 tbsp oil
- A teaspoon of dried oregano
- A teaspoon of ground garlic
- A sliced green pepper
- One celery stick, chopped
- Ripe, black olives to taste (sliced)

Directions:

- To a bag add flour, salt, and pepper. Shake the rabbit pieces in the bag to coat thoroughly with flour. Sauté in a skillet until golden brown.
- To the skillet and rabbit, add the remaining ingredients, except the olives. Cover and simmer on low heat for one hour or until the meat turn tender. Stir black olives in and simmer for an additional 10 minutes.
- Serve with noodles or rice.

Bacon-Wrapped Rabbit Loin

Bacon makes everything tastier. You'll only need three ingredients for this recipe, but if you want extra flavor try basting the loins with your favorite barbecue sauce whilst grilling.

Serving Size: Makes four servings.

Cook Time: 60 minutes

Nutritional Information:

Calories	Carbs	Fat	Protein
217	0g	11g	27g

Ingredients

- One pound of rabbit loin
- 6 slices of bacon
- Salt and pepper to taste

Directions:

- Season loins with salt and pepper and wrap with pieces of bacon. Use toothpicks to secure the bacon if needed.
- Preheat a grill to medium heat. Place the loins directly on the grill and cook until an internal temperature of 160° has been reached. Turn the loins twice during the grilling process.
- Allow the loins to rest for five minutes before serving with sides of your choice.

Rabbit Keeper's Pie

This simple, mash-topped stew is perfect for those days when you crave comfort food that won't sit a lifetime on the hips. Indulgent and filling, this pie is perfect to drive the cold (and blues) away.

Serving Size: Makes four servings.

Cook Time: 140 minutes

Nutritional Information:

Calories	Carbs	Fat	Protein
435	31g	21g	26g

Ingredients:

- 1.5 lbs. of rabbit, deboned and cut into pieces
- 1 tbsp oil
- A large, chopped onion
- 2 carrots, chopped
- 2 oz butter
- Half a pound of venison sausages, removed from the skins
- 2 tbsp flour
- 1 tbsp tomato puree
- Half a cup of red wine
- 2 cups of stock (chicken, beef or vegetable)
- 1 tbsp Worcestershire sauce (can be substituted with soy sauce)
- A bay leaf
- 2 tsp dried thyme
- 14 oz of potato, peeled and chopped (can use sweet potato as an alternative)
- One pound of chopped mixed root vegetables of your choice
- 2 tbsp of milk

Directions:

- Melt half of the butter and oil in a large pan. Add the onion and carrots and cook until soft (roughly 10 minutes). Add rabbit and sausage to the pan and turn up the heat. Cook until the meat has browned.
- To the pan, add flour and tomato puree. Stir in until fully incorporated. Proceed to add wine, stock, Worcestershire sauce, bay leaf, and thyme. Bring the mixture to a simmer and reduce the heat. Cook covered for an hour, after which, you should remove the lid and cook for an additional 15 minutes uncovered to thicken the sauce.
- Place potatoes and vegetables in a large saucepan and cover with water. Bring to a boil and cook for 20 minutes (or until the vegetables are tender). Drain the contents and mash with seasoning, milk, and the remainder of the butter.
- Heat the oven to 430°. Tip the contents of the meat pan into an ovenproof dish and spoon the mash over. Don't worry about creating a smooth surface with the mash, the "hills and valleys" created by the mash will add additional texture and rustic charm to the dish. Sprinkle

the remaining thyme over the top and bake for 45 minutes or until golden brown.

Rabbit Hotpot With Mushrooms

This take on a Lancashire hotpot only uses a few ingredients and is bound to impress. This easy-to-make recipe just adds to the versatility of rabbit meat.

Serving Size: Makes four servings.

Cook Time: 105 minutes

Nutritional Information:

Calories	Carbs	Fat	Protein
544	58g	18g	42g

Ingredients

- 3 tbsp oil
- 3 lbs. of oven-ready rabbit (legs, shoulder, and loins are best to use)
- 10 oz of Portabellini mushrooms, thinly sliced
- 2 lbs. of thinly sliced potatoes
- 3 large onions, halved and thinly sliced
- 1 tbsp chopped rosemary
- 2 cups of stock (vegetable or chicken)

Directions:

- Heat the oven to 365°. In a deep ovenproof casserole dish, heat the oil and add the rabbit. Brown the meat and lift the meat into a plate. Add mushrooms to the same casserole dish and give it a quick stir-fry. Scoop the mushrooms out of the dish and remove the casserole from the heat.
- Layer half of the potatoes into the casserole. Remember to season as you layer! Top with half of the onions, mushrooms, and rosemary. Add all of the rabbit. On top of the rabbit, build layers with the remaining onion, mushroom, and rosemary. The final layer should be potatoes.
- Pour stock over and gently brush the top layer of potatoes with oil.
- Return the casserole to the heat and bring it to a boil, cover, and pop in the oven for one hour. Remove the lid and turn the oven up to 430°. Bake for an additional 30 minutes, or until the top has browned.
- Serve with your favorite cooked greens.

Rabbit Au Vin

This French-inspired stew combines shallots, carrots, and bacon into a decadent family feast! Rabbit turns extra tender and flavorful when cooked with wine.

Serving Size: Makes six servings.

Cook Time: 150 minutes

Nutritional Information:

Calories	Carbs	Fat	Protein
600	12g	24g	65g

Ingredients:

- 4 lbs. of rabbit, jointed
- 15 oz of shallots
- 2 sliced onions
- 2 sliced celery sticks
- 7 oz streaky bacon
- 2 tbsp flour
- 2 tbsp of butter
- 1 tbsp oil
- 2 cups of red wine (full-bodied works best)
- 13 oz of stock (chicken or vegetable)
- 2 bay leaves
- Thyme to taste

- 10 oz of mushrooms (button mushrooms works best)

Directions:

- Blanch the shallots in boiling water for 5 minutes. Drain and peel. Heat a large, heat-proof casserole dish and add the bacon. Fry until the fat has been rendered from the meat. Tip the vegetables into the bacon fat and cook for 10 minutes until they start to soften. Ladle the vegetables into a bowl and keep them aside for now.
- Toss the rabbit with flour. Using the same casserole dish, heat half of the butter and oil and proceed to brown the meat.
- Heat a large, wide flameproof casserole dish, then add the lardons. Fry for 5 mins or until the fat has run from the meat, then tip in the vegetables and cook for 10 mins until golden and starting to soften. Tip it into a bowl. Once all the rabbit has been browned, remove it from the dish and add wine to deglaze the pan. Allow the liquid to reduce by a third.
- Return the rabbit and vegetables to the casserole and pour the stock in. Stir the herbs and let the mixture simmer, partially covered

for up to two hours (or until the meat falls off the bone).

- Finish the dish by heating butter and cooking the mushrooms with salt, pepper, and some thyme in a pan on high heat. Spoon the mushrooms over the stew and serve.

These recipes demonstrate how easy it can be to cook with rabbit meat. From homely comfort foods to refined dishes, there seems to be no limit to how one can use rabbit meat. Rabbits' versatility does not end in the kitchen. They are money-generating machines to some breeders. In the next chapter, we'll explore different ways rabbits can be utilized to generate income at a level beyond offsetting feed costs.

9

GENERATING MONEY WITH RABBITS

The biggest advantage to raising rabbits is that almost all parts of the animal can be used to turn a profit. In these questionable economic times, every penny counts, and the frugal and informed homesteader can make money in surprising ways with a rabbitry. Keep in mind that that income from a single stream may not be much, but when combined with other income streams, rabbit keepers may find that they are supplementing their income beyond offsetting the cost of feed or breeding stock.

Selling Rabbit Meat

Rabbit meat is quite popular throughout the world, but it has not gained as much traction as it deserves in the United States. For the entrepreneurial spirit, this means there is a potential market to benefit from. Keep in mind that you may need to educate potential customers on the virtues of rabbit meat. It is a white meat that is superior to chicken in nutritional value. Rabbitries also tend to have far smaller carbon footprints than chicken farms. These characteristics make it desirable meat for the health-conscious individual and those who are environmentally aware. Usually, rabbit meat is served in high-end restaurants, but it can be hard to find rabbit meat at your local butcher.

If you are confident in the kitchen, you might consider selling barbecued rabbits to local consumers, market-places, restaurants, events, or food stalls as a way to generate income. It's a great way to attract loyal customers, especially if the rabbit is mouthwatering. This might be an appealing option for those consumers who love rabbit meat but are not confident in cooking it. Keep in mind that food industry standards apply when following this route.

Larger-scale operations might consider opening a slaughterhouse. Generally, rabbit keepers find it chal-lenging to find a butcher that will process their rabbits, so opening a slaughterhouse may be a good option. When opening a slaughterhouse, please adhere to local and state requirements for these facilities.

Rabbit meat is a delicacy, so the price you can get per pound will reflect this. It is not unreasonable to ask for up to $7.00 per pound, regardless if the meat is intended for human consumption or sold as dog food. Due to rabbit meat being so difficult to obtain at your local grocer, you'll likely get the price you are asking, granted it is not exorbitant.

Selling Pelts

Many meat rabbit breeds are dual-purpose and can be raised for their pelts and meat. The hide is a byproduct of the harvesting process, but it can be turned into something beautiful by those who are creatively inclined. Pelts can be used to make clothes, dolls, handbags, and other goodies. Tanning rabbit hides can be tricky, but this topic will be covered in the next chapter. Pelts can bring you anywhere from $1.00 to $30.00 a pelt, depending on the breed and age of the rabbit, how well it has been tanned, the size of the pelt, and the color of the fur. Some fur colors are more desirable than others, so it is worth asking around.

An alternative is to sell the fur as fiber. This is done by shearing or hand-plucking the fur from long-haired breeds like the Angora Rabbit. As a luxury item, rabbit fur is used to create soft and silky products, making it very desirable for crafters and commercial operations. Keep in mind that fur rabbits require greater measures of care than most meat breeds. Beautiful fiber takes a lot of work and long-haired breeds tend to have matted fur when the breeder does not care for them properly. Rabbit fiber can be sold online, in flea markets, to yarn shops, spinners, and many other places. The condition and color of the fiber will determine how much money you'll get from it. Generally, Angora fiber can be sold for upwards of $7.00 an ounce.

Turn Poop Into Profit With Manure

Rabbits are poop factories. Depending on the size and breed, a single rabbit can produce two pounds of potential manure a day! Times that by the number of rabbits that you have, and you've got a potential steady income source. Rabbit manure is a wonderful fertilizer as it is rich in nitrogen. Unlike commercial fertilizers, they can be applied directly to plants without burning vegetation. That's a bonus for farmers, garden enthusiasts, homesteaders, and garden centers alike! The best part? You don't have to wait months before using rabbit manure, as one would when using fertilizer from other animal sources. This means rabbit keepers have a potential income source from day one of their rabbitry.

Rabbit manure sold as fertilizer can fetch up to $45 for a 40-lb bag, but this is not the norm. Usually, rabbit keepers give the manure away, because they want to be rid of it, losing out on a potential income stream in the process. Of course, you can ask more if the manure has been composted with worms or aged. The price you'll ask for the fertilizer will depend on your location as well.

Vermicomposting helps to reduce the odor of manure and the worms can be sold to bait shops, fishermen, individuals who use composting bins, and exotic pet shops that need a steady supply of worms to feed their lizards. Earthworms and nightcrawlers can easily be sold for $31.00 per pound, but keep in mind that worms don't weigh much. A pound of worms will take some time to produce.

Selling Live Rabbits

Most rabbits make wonderful pets, which opens yet another avenue for income. Some breeders choose to sell their rabbits directly to customers, while others approach their local pet store to become rabbit suppliers. Just remember, pet stores may be able to push larger numbers but are typically unwilling to pay more than $15.00 per rabbit. If going the pet store route, mull it over carefully! Pet stores don't typically care about the breed of rabbit or pedigree, they'll still offer you less than what the rabbit is worth.

With some clever marketing, especially around Easter and fair time, live rabbits can be sold for anywhere between \$20.00 and \$100.00, depending on the breed and condition of the animal. Selling live rabbits directly to the customer has one added benefit that's absolutely heartwarming: you'll get to witness countless children choose their first pet. Kits are kid-magnets so hanging flyers locally or advertising on Google when your rabbits have kindled is a good way to get the word out.

To make the most out of selling live rabbits, the breeder must pick the correct breed and color from the start. Rare breeds and pedigreed rabbits sell for a higher price. Keep records of your rabbits up to the third or fourth generation and never sell a rabbit that looks unwell.

How Many Generations Should a Pedigree Record?

At a very minimum, three generations should be recorded. At its most basic iteration, a pedigree provides the family tree of a given rabbit. Three generations starting from the individual's great-grandparents to the grandparents and parents should be accounted for in order to consider the record as a full pedigree. A partial pedigree would have information missing. A full pedigree needs to have all the information on hand that is required for registration. This includes the rabbit's name, tattoo number, birth date, weight, color variety and pattern, and any grand championship numbers.

Tattooing a Rabbit

In the United States, tattooing is the only accepted method to identify rabbits used for breeding and showing purposes. The legible tattoo in the rabbit's ear provides a permanent identification mark. Rabbits that are shown at the American Rabbit Breeders Association typically have a tattoo in the left ear. Tattoos in the right ear can only be placed there by the Rabbit Breeders Association registrar.

Selling Pinkies

This option is not for the squeamish. "Pinkies" or newborn kits can be sold to exotic pet stores and snake owners as a source of food. Don't worry, you don't need to sacrifice live kits for this purpose! Sometimes a litter has kits that won't survive, or that have been still-born. In large a rabbitry, there will be rabbits that abandon their kits, or there may be instances where kits simply can't be fostered and die. When you spot a dead kit, it can be collected and frozen, granted it has not been dead for too long. Once you have enough, they can be sold. It might help to think of yourself as a "rabbit mortician" and the freezer that the kits are being stored in as the "rabbit morgue". Still, this is not a route many feel comfortable taking, and many rabbit keepers simply bury or dispose of dead pinkies. For the morbidly curious, pinkies can be sold for around $3.00 each.

Take Rabbits to the Internet

Those who have a knack for teaching and a passion for rabbits can provide classes (in person or online) on how to take care of rabbits. Many new rabbit owners do not realize the extent of care that a rabbit requires, so these classes will be helpful and can cover a variety of topics from meat and fiber production to disease prevention and litter training! Your imagination is the only limit here. Alternatively, you could create rabbit care videos for TikTok, YouTube, or Instagram or simply live stream the cuteness of your rabbits. Remember to link all your social platforms and websites to generate a decent digital footprint.

Many rabbitries have a dedicated website or blog which they use to cover rabbit-related topics like fiber-plucking, meat production, pet care, or raising rabbits on a budget. Having a storefront with an Amazon affiliate page is a good way to monetize your website. Affiliate marketing can be used to monetize any rabbit-related videos that you produce as well. Remember to add an email subscription option to your blog or website so your loyal customers can keep abreast of the latest goings-on.

Some breeders have beautiful, intricate rabbitries and frequently design these structures for new rabbit keepers or sell the plans online. As you can see, there's a plethora of ways you can generate an income from rabbits, all you need is passion, a touch of imagination, and a dash of marketing savvy. Before long, you'll be able to enjoy multiple income streams from one well-designed and planned rabbitry.

PELTS AND TANNING

The practice of tanning hides can be traced to ancient Sumeria thousands of years ago (Manchee, 2017). Ancient tanners did not have a glamorous role, and tanneries were confined to the outskirts of settlements for good reason: they stank to the high heavens! Tanning hides in the ancient way that took months to complete. The taxing work required tanners to soften the skin and scrape fat from the hides, whereafter it would be softened in a bacteria-infested concoction. Tanning hides was undoubtedly the toughest job in antiquity, but thankfully modern chemicals make the process so much easier (and a lot less smelly).

Many modern homesteaders are not sure what to do with their rabbit pelts, so they simply assign them to the compost heap. Tanning hides is not a complicated process and contrary to popular belief, small pelt tanning is not a time-consuming process. Nor is it expensive! It's a different story if you were to tan the hide of a cow, deer, or another large animal, but rabbits are once again the unsung heroes of frugal living.

Tanning is the process of preserving the hide, turning it into leather, and making the skin soft and pliable. Rabbit hide is soft and warm, making it an excellent material to use for gloves, hats, and blankets, or can be used as a lining in jackets and coats to keep the cold at bay. People who spend extended hours outside in cold weather and snow, such as hunters, ranchers, and construction workers, will have use for a lined coat.

Rabbits have a multitude of fur colors and patterns, which can turn hide tanning into an exciting project. Novices need not shy away. With a little practice and some knowledge, anyone can learn this ancient skill. What follows is a closer look at a commonly used tanning process. These are not the only ways to tan hides and novices are encouraged to research their chosen methods thoroughly. It is advisable to steer clear from vegetable and oil tanning methods as they are not suited for preserving rabbit skin.

TANNING HIDES FOR BEGINNERS

Freshly flayed hides are referred to as "green skin". As soon as you've skinned the carcass, don't dump the pelt in the offal bucket. Soak it in cold water while you finish with the carcass.

Preparing Green Hides

When you are free from butchering duties, thoroughly rinse the hide in clean cold water. The goal is to cool it as quickly as possible. Don't worry about fatty deposits at this stage, just get the pelt cold and free from the blood for now. Any blood that remains on the skin will turn into ugly brown stains during the tanning process, ruining a potentially beautiful hide. It may be tempting to reach for soaps or detergents to help wash away the blood, but this is not necessary. You'll make double work for yourself as you'll need to ensure that all traces of the soap are rinsed away, as they can spoil the leather during the tanning process. I've heard that some hobbyist tanners simply pop the flayed skins in their washers on a gentle cycle, but this is not advised. Fatty deposits and fur will clog the drain hose.

Clean hides can be frozen and processed later, dried on a stretcher, or salted and dried. Before freezing pelts, make sure that all body heat has dissipated from the skins and that there is no excess water. Wrap the hides in freezer paper or store them in airtight containers to protect them from freezer burn and prevent the hides from drying out.

First Tanning Solution

After the pelts have been cleaned and cooled (or defrosted), the tanning process can begin. You'll need to gather the following supplies:

- Plastic container (four gallons or larger).
- Two gallons of room temperature water.
- Either Tanning Solution A or Tanning Solution B, but not both.

Tanning Solution A: Salt/Alum

Take one cup of coarse salt (non-iodized) and combine it with one cup of common alum. It produces a whiter and softer leather with a feel akin to suede.

Tanning Solution B: Salt/Acid

Use one pound of granulated salt and four ounces of battery acid (Kellogg, 2022). If using full-strength sulfuric acid, use one ounce. Always wear protective gear when working with chemicals.

When you've gathered the supplies, pour the water into the container. Fully incorporate the tanning solution.

Be careful when adding chemicals to water, you don't want them to splash. Carefully lower each hide into the solution (which is now known as a pickle) and gently stir with a wooden stick. A sturdy broomstick will get the job done.

The pelts need to remain in the brine for two days. Keep them at room temperature and stir twice a day (or more). Pelts that float to the top can be weighed down with a clean rock.

When two days have passed, the pelts can be removed from the brine. Reserve the mixture, though. You still need it. Squeeze excess brine from the pelts and rinse thoroughly with cold water.

Fleshing

Think of fleshing as the process of "uncovering" the leather. Fatty tissue and flesh are removed to expose the derma (the actual leather) to the tanning solution. The under tissue is clearly defined in rabbit skins and can be peeled off after the first soak in a tanning solution. Skillful tanners can peel the under tissue off in one piece.

The hide can be scraped with a steak knife to remove under tissue from difficult areas, such as the belly and legs. When handling the knife, you'll need a balanced touch: the goal is to remove fatty tissue, but not to expose any root hairs. After all of the under tissue is removed the hides should be rinsed in cool water. Squeeze the excess liquid from the hide.

Second Tanning Solution

Add more tanning solution to the reserved brine. Use the same solution in the same quantities that you used for the first soak. After the tanning solution is fully incorporated, add the pelts to the liquid and thoroughly coat in the pickle. The skins need to soak at room temperature for a week, stirred at least twice a day.

Testing For Leather

After a week, you can test for tanning completion by boiling a small piece of hide for a few minutes in water. There should be little to no change to the skin. If it curls up and turns hard and rubbery, the pelts are not ready yet and will need to soak longer. When one pelt passes the test, you can safely remove all the pelts from the pickle. Squeeze out the excess liquid and begin the drying process.

At this point, the pickle can be discarded. Take care to dispose of it in such a manner that animals and drinking water won't be affected.

Drying

After squeezing excess pickle from the pelts, wash them thoroughly with a mild detergent. An inexpensive shampoo will work beautifully and leave the fur soft, clean, and smelling nice. Rinse the hide several times in lukewarm water and squeeze excess liquid from it. The pelts are ready to be hung now. When hanging pelts, never expose them to direct sunlight or heat as they'll shrink and become brittle. Always hang them in the shade. It may take some time for them to dry (up to 48 hours).

Machine Fluffing (Optional)

Check on the hides regularly. When they are touch dry (just barely damp), toss the hides into an electric dryer for 15–45 mins. Don't use any heat. Machine fluffing makes the hide easier to work with.

Breaking The Hide

The pelt is not usable yet. It needs to be worked. In ancient times, animal skins would have been beaten, chewed, rubbed, and anointed with oils to make and keep them flexible. There is an easier way though. Partially dried hides can be stretched. You want to work a hide that is dry to the touch, but still limp. Simply pull the skin of the damp pelt in all directions. It is easiest to work in small sections. Use a firm grip as you pull the leather, but be careful not to tear it. If the leather becomes too hard, moisten the area with a wet sponge. Continue breaking the skin until the pelt remains soft as it dries. Once the hide is fully broken it can be tacked to a frame or board to dry flat.

Rounding-Off and Storage

After the hide has been softened, the fur should be brushed. A hand brush works well. Massage mink oil, obtainable at shoe stores and online, into the skin side of the pelt. Mink oil will leave the leather and your hands feeling soft. Buff the skin side with fine sand-paper or pumice stone after the oil massage. Buffing is optional, but it gives the leather a velvety feel. The pelts are ready for storage now.

Never store leather in airtight containers. It is best to store them in a cardboard box, away from direct sunlight.

Preventing Taint

Even though the tanning process is simple enough, it can still be tricky to learn. The secret to successfully tan hides does not lie in the chemicals that you use, but in the effort that you exert to work the hides. Each piece of leather is different and it is not uncommon for something to go wrong with one or more skins when working in batches.

The most common problem you may encounter is bare patches that appear on the leather. This happens when the fur falls off, leaving bare patches behind. This is called taint and is the result of bacterial growth and skin decay. Folds, wrinkles, and areas of the skin that were not thoroughly exposed to tanning solutions are the culprits here. This can be prevented in three ways:

- Ensure that the ingredients used for the tanning solution are of high quality and were properly dissolved.
- Stir the pelts frequently during the pickling process.
- Don't store pelts in the pickle at temperatures that exceed 80°.

Sections with taint can be trimmed away when creating leather products.

BEST MEAT BREEDS FOR FUR

There are roughly 305 different breeds of domestic rabbits across the world (Wikipedia Contributors, 2019). Many rabbit breeds can be deemed multipurpose breeds and are kept for meat and fur production. With that being said, let's take a brief look at some of the best meat and fur breeds.

Altex Rabbit

This commercial breed gains weight rapidly and has a mature weight of 13 pounds, making it a great meat rabbit. The Altex is known to be docile and makes good pets. Shedding is not much of an issue with this breed and it has short, white fur. They have black markings on their noses and gray ears. These rabbits are quite sociable and get along with other rabbits. Litter sizes are moderate that can range between four and eight kits per kindling.

Belgian Hare

Belgian Hares have long, slim hind legs and bodies. Fur color is usually red with black ticking, but tan and chestnut-colored fur are out there too. Does weigh between eight and nine pounds, while bucks tip the scales at six to eight pounds. A litter can range from four to eight kits, but they have a slow growth rate. These rabbits have a good disposition.

Beveren

This breed is known to have highly prized blue pelts, but other color variants include lilac, white, black and brown. Bear in mind that not all color variants are recognized by the American Rabbit Breeders Association. White Beverens are quite striking with their brilliant coats and blue eyes, while blue Beverens tend to have blue-gray eyes. These rabbits are a rare breed and have an even temperament with a good meat-to-bone ratio. Does can weigh up to 12 pounds. Bucks can reach a weight of 11 pounds.

Dutch Rabbit

This small rabbit has excellent maternal instincts. Does are known to foster kits when needed (Ahsan, 2014). The Dutch Rabbit is a friendly breed and the litters can be quite large, up to a dozen kits per kindling. Does weigh around six pounds, while bucks hover between four and five pounds. Their coat has distinct markings.

Harlequin

This large and colorful rabbit breed has an excellent meat-to-bone ratio. Does' weight varies between six and nine pounds, and bucks tend to weigh a touch less. They are fast-growing and can be butchered at the 10-week mark. Harlequins are good-natured and produce up to 10 kits per litter. Their fur has markings that give it a striped resemblance. The pelt of this breed is often used for creating warm outerwear.

Himalayan Rabbit

This medium-sized rabbit has a white coat. Color points can be spotted on the ears, feet, and nose and range between lilac, blue and dark brown. This gives the breed a similar appearance to the Californian rabbit. Does weigh six pounds and bucks average at five pounds. These rabbits are typically raised for their pelts and make good meat rabbits. Litters are large, up to 12 kits per kindling.

Always research your chosen breeds carefully to ensure a good fit for your rabbitry.

CONCLUSION

At this point, you know everything you need to confidently raise rabbits! One of the biggest reasons people turn to rabbit meat is because it is packed with nutrients. Apart from protein, rabbits are rich in vitamin B-12 and selenium. These vitamins play an important role in keeping our metabolism and immune systems healthy (Wendt, 2022). Raising rabbits for meat is an exciting adventure, one which provides advantages that stretches beyond a well-stocked freezer. With a little research and planning, rabbits can be raised successfully by practically anyone with suitable space.

Appropriate housing is the first and most important step to address when venturing to raise rabbits. They'll need to be protected from predators, the elements, and excessive temperatures. Suitable sleeping, nesting, feeding, and play areas will need to be provided. The more space you can give your rabbits, the happier they'll be.

I can't stress enough how important it is to research the rabbit breeds you'd like to breed with. Each breed is unique and some breeds have very specific care requirements. If you've never raised rabbits before, I'd encourage you to try New Zealand Whites or any of the beginner-friendly breeds mentioned in this book. Try to select the breed that will best satisfy your goal for the lowest feed cost. A well-run rabbitry can practically pay for its own feed and provide the opportunity for multiple income streams for breeders. So, treat your rabbitry like a small startup, you'd be surprised at how effortlessly it could scale.

Now that you have all the tools needed to confidently start a rabbitry, go out there and use it! The internet is filled with false information and bad advice, so if this book helped answer your rabbit questions, please feel free to leave a review. I look forward to hearing about your rabbit-raising adventures!

GLOSSARY

Alum: A chemical compound used in the tanning process. Alum is usually a hydrated double-sulfate salt of aluminum and is used to produce a soft, white leather.

Broken fur:

Broken refers to the pattern on the fur. Rabbits that are one color (only white or only black) are referred to as solid colored, but if there is a speck of a different color it's called broken.

Buck: Male rabbit.

Crocks: Water dishes for rabbits, usually made from porcelain or heavy plastic.

Colony Raising: Rabbits are raised with other rabbits in a small herd. The herd is usually housed in a pen and rabbits can freely interact with each other.

Commercial Breeds: Breeds of rabbits that are commonly available like the New Zealand Whites. These breeds typically have red eyes.

Cull: To remove a rabbit from your breeding stock, either by dispatching it or by keeping it in a separate enclosure.

Cuniculture: The agricultural practice of raising rabbits as livestock for meat, fur, or wool.

Dewlap: It is a fold of skin and fur from which the doe gathers fur for the kits' nest. In some breeds, the dewlap is located near the doe's neck.

Dispatch: To humanely kill a rabbit.

Doe: Female rabbit

Fall Off: When a buck ejaculates, he falls off to the side of the doe.

Fiber: Rabbit hairs that are collected for the production of materials.

Flaying: The act of removing the skin from an animal.

Fleshing: The act of scraping fat and flesh from the hide during the tanning process.

Fryer: Young, processed rabbit that is under five months old. Best suited for frying or as a chicken replacement.

Green Hides: Hides that have not been treated with tanning solution yet.

Grow Outs: Weaned rabbits that are six to eight weeks old.

Herd: A group of rabbits in a rabbitry.

Heritage Breeds: Breeds of rabbits that are recognized by their dark eyes and selectively bred for desirable traits. Harlequins and the Silver Fox breeds are two examples of heritage breeds. These breeds tend to be a bit harder to find than commercial breeds.

Hopper Popper: Tool used to dispatch rabbits humanely.

Hutch: Compact form of rabbit housing meant to house rabbits separately. Hutches are versatile and can be used to house rabbits indoors, and outdoors or can be connected to runs.

Hybrid Breeds: Crossbreeds that result when a commercial breed is mated with a heritage breed. Successful cross breeding requires intimate knowledge of the rabbit breeds that are being mated as many complications can arise from indiscriminate breeding.

Kit: Baby rabbit.

Kindle: To give birth.

Kindling Box: A wooden box constructed for does to bear their litters in.

Lift: When a doe is receptive to breeding.

Litter: Kits from the same pregnancy.

Myxomatosis: A highly infectious disease in rabbits that is caused by a viral infection. The disease spreads quickly in herds and can destroy entire rabbitries if no precautionary measures are taken.

Offal: Parts to be discarded when slaughtering a rabbit. Offal includes intestines, stomach, lungs, and other bits deemed unfit for human consumption.

Pedigree: A record showing the lineage of an animal. A minimum of three generations need to be recorded before the record is considered a valid pedigree.

Pellets: Commercially produced food for rabbits, typically made from an assortment of grasses and grains.

Pickle: Liquid tanning solution is sometimes referred to as "pickle."

Pinkies: Newborn kits. The name is derived from their pink and hairless appearance.

Process / Harvest: To skin and gut a rabbit.

Quarantine: To separate an individual from the main herd.

Rabbitry: Housing for rabbits.

Rabbit Hemorrhagic Disease Virus: Viral disease in rabbits considered endemic in many countries. Precautionary measures need to be taken to protect rabbits from the virus.

Rabbit Run: An exercise space, usually attached to a hutch, intended to provide rabbits space to safely exercise and play.

Roaster: Older, processed rabbit that is over five months of age. Best suited for slow cooking and roasting.

Rollback Fur: Rollback fur returns to their original position when stroked "against the grain" or in the opposite direction in which the fur grows.

Tanning: The process of preserving animal hides by means of applying chemicals.

Tanning Solution: Chemical solution used to preserve hides.

Taint: Areas of tarnish that settles in on poorly preserved hides. Taint is characterized by hair loss and bald patches. Areas where taint occurs are cut out and discarded when the leather is used for garments and crafts.

REFERENCES

Ahsan, F. (2014, April 4). *17 Best Meat Rabbit Breeds for Homesteads*. The Self-Sufficient Living. https://theselfsufficientliving.com/best-meat-rabbit-breeds/

Alyssa. (2019, October 11). *Commercial Meat Rabbit Growth Rates*. Homestead Rabbits. https://homesteadrabbits.com/meat-rabbit-growth-rates/

Carter, L. (2019, April 1). *How To Protect Rabbits from Predators*. Rabbit Care Tips. https://www.rabbitcaretips.com/protect-rabbits-from-predators/#:~:text=Give%20your%20rabbit%20at%20least

Cheeke, P. R., Lukefahr, S. D., & Patton, N. M. (2000). *Rabbit Production*. Interstate Publishers.

Elliott, P. (2019, August 8). *How to Care for Newborn Rabbits: 11 Steps (with Pictures)*. WikiHow. https://www.wikihow.com/Care-for-Newborn-Rabbits#:~:text=Kits%20are%20born%20without%20fur

Hall, R. (n.d.). *Recognized Breeds – ARBA*. Www.printfriendly.com. Retrieved August 3, 2022, from https://www.printfriendly.com/p/g/XjTmst

Humanity Development Library 2.0. (n.d.). *A complete handbook on back-yard and commercial rabbit production: The rabbitry and its equipment: Nest boxes*. Humanity Development Library 2.0. Retrieved July 30, 2022, from http://www.nzdl.org/cgi-bin/library.cgi?e=d-00000-00---off-0hdl--00-0----0-10-0---0---0direct-10---4-------0-1l--11-en-50---20-about---00-0-1-00-0-0-11-1-0utfZz-8-00&a=d&c=hdl&cl=CL3.43&d=HASH8ef3addce883f5d4bcb708.7.5

Irvine, K. (2019a, January 27). *American Chinchilla Rabbit – Everything You Need to Know*. Domesticanimalbreeds.com. https://domesticanimalbreeds.com/american-chinchilla-rabbit-breed-everything-you-need-to-know/

Irvine, K. (2019b, February 4). *New Zealand Rabbit – Everything You*

Need to Know. Domesticanimalbreeds.com. https://domesticanimal breeds.com/new-zealand-rabbit-everything-you-need-to-know/

Irvine, K. (2019c, February 4). *Rex Rabbit – Everything You Need to Know.* Domesticanimalbreeds.com. https://domesticanimalbreeds.com/rex-rabbit-everything-you-need-to-know/

Irvine, K. (2019d, February 4). *Search Results for "Palomino."* Domesticanimalbreeds.com. https://domesticanimalbreeds.com/?s=Palomino

Irvine, K. (2019e, February 4). *Silver Fox Rabbit – Everything You Need to Know.* Domesticanimalbreeds.com. https://domesticanimalbreeds.com/silver-fox-rabbit-everything-you-need-to-know/

Irvine, K. (2019f, February 7). *Californian Rabbit – Everything You Need to Know.* Domesticanimalbreeds.com. https://domesticanimal breeds.com/californian-rabbit-everything-you-need-to-know/

Irvine, K. (2019g, February 7). *Champagne D'Argent Rabbit – Everything You Need to Know.* Domesticanimalbreeds.com. https://domesticani malbreeds.com/champagne-dargent-rabbit-everything-you-need-to-know/

Irvine, K. (2019h, February 7). *Florida White Rabbit – Everything You Need to Know.* Domesticanimalbreeds.com. https://domesticanimal breeds.com/florida-white-rabbit-everything-you-need-to-know/

Irvine, K. (2019i, March 2). *Satin Rabbit – Everything You Need to Know.* Domesticanimalbreeds.com. https://domesticanimalbreeds.com/satin-rabbit-everything-you-need-to-know/

Jakob, R. (2020, April 15). *10 Best Meat Rabbit Breeds in the World (with Pictures).* Pet Keen. https://petkeen.com/best-meat-rabbit-breeds/

Kellogg, K. (2022, January 4). *How to Tan a Rabbit Hide – Mother Earth News.* Mother Earth News – the Original Guide to Living Wisely. https://www.motherearthnews.com/diy/how-to-tan-a-rabbit-hide-zmaz83jfzraw/#:~:text=Put%20the%20pelts%20in%20the

Klein, N. (2019, June 12). *Meat Rabbit Breed Selection | Hostile Hare Rabbits for Homestesading.* Hostile Hare. https://hostilehare.com/meat-rabbit-breed-selection/

KW Cages. (n.d.). *Rabbit Nest Boxes 101.* KW Cages. Retrieved August 1,

2022, from https://www.kwcages.com/rabbit-nest-boxes-101#:~:text=Keep%20in%20mind%20that%20the

Manchee, S. (2017, June 5). *A Quick History Of The Leather Tanning Industry*. Blackstock Leather. https://blackstockleather.com/history-of-the-leather-tanning-industry/#:~:text=Between%2012%2C000%20and%206%2C000%20years

Mccune, K. (2022). *How Long Does It Take To Raise A Rabbit For Meat?* Family Farm Livestock. https://familyfarmlivestock.com/how-long-does-it-take-to-raise-a-rabbit-for-meat/

McVean, A. (2018, March 31). *Rabbits Eat Their Own Poop*. Office for Science and Society. https://www.mcgill.ca/oss/article/did-you-know/rabbits-eat-their-own-poop

Mitchell, S. C. (2018, September 17). *What's the Perfect Rabbit Cage Setup? | petMD*. Petmd.com. https://www.petmd.com/rabbit/care/whats-perfect-rabbit-cage-setup

MSD Veterinary Manual. (n.d.). *Management of Rabbits - Exotic and Laboratory Animals*. MSD Veterinary Manual. Retrieved August 13, 2022, from https://www.msdvetmanual.com/

Ni Direct Government Services. (2015, November 20). *Protecting rabbits from pain, injury and disease*. Nidirect. https://www.nidirect.gov.uk/articles/protecting-rabbits-pain-injury-and-disease

Pieper, A. (2019, October 1). *A Complete Guide to Breeding Rabbits for Beginners*. MorningChores. https://morningchores.com/breeding-rabbits/#:~:text=Rabbits%20should%20not%20be%20bred

Rabbit Hole Hay. (2019, February 1). *Should I Have My Rabbit Use a Water Bowl or Water Bottle?* Rabbit Hole Hay. https://www.rabbitholehay.com/blogs/rabbit-hole-hay-blog/should-i-have-my-rabbit-use-a-water-bowl-or-a-water-bottle

Rise and Shine Rabbitry. (2012, October 21). *WHAT BREED OF RABBIT TO RAISE FOR MEAT?* Rise and Shine Rabbitry. https://riseandshinerabbitry.com/2012/10/21/what-breed-of-rabbit-to-raise-for-meat/

Steenekamp, K. (n.d.). *Diseases in Rabbits - South Africa*. Southafrica.co.za. Retrieved August 7, 2022, from https://southafrica.co.za/diseases-in-rabbits.html#:~:text=South%20Africa%20is%20one%20of

Stone, T. (n.d.). *Choosing Rabbit Food Bowls & Dispensers*. The Rabbit House. http://www.therabbithouse.com/equipment/rabbit-food-bowl.asp

The Humane Society of the United States. (2022). *Where to get your new rabbit*. The Humane Society of the United States. https://www.humanesociety.org/resources/where-get-your-new-rabbit

Wendt, T. (2022, June 3). *What Are the Health Benefits of Rabbit Meat?* WebMD. https://www.webmd.com/diet/health-benefits-rabbit-meat

Wikipedia Contributors. (2019, March 27). *List of rabbit breeds*. Wikipedia; Wikimedia Foundation. https://en.wikipedia.org/wiki/List_of_rabbit_breeds

RABBIT RECIPES. (2022, June 10). The Rabbitry Center. Retrieved September 13, 2022, from https://therabbitrycenter.com/rabbit-recipes/

Made in United States
Orlando, FL
28 March 2025

59944798R00120